J. P. (Julia Parker) Dabney

Songs of Destiny and Others

J. P. (Julia Parker) Dabney

Songs of Destiny and Others

ISBN/EAN: 9783743313187

Manufactured in Europe, USA, Canada, Australia, Japa

Cover: Foto ©Thomas Meinert / pixelio.de

Manufactured and distributed by brebook publishing software (www.brebook.com)

J. P. (Julia Parker) Dabney

Songs of Destiny and Others

SONGS OF DESTINY
AND OTHERS

BY

JULIA P. DABNEY

Author of "Poor Chola," "Little Daughter of
the Sun," etc.

NEW YORK
E. P. DUTTON & COMPANY
31 WEST TWENTY-THIRD STREET
1898

CONTENTS.

Songs of Destiny.

	PAGE
I.—EARTH-TOUCH	1
II.—FIRE-BAPTISM	17
III.—STAR-MIST	20
IV.—DESTINY	30

Miscellaneous Poems.

MIRACLE	36
OF MY STAR	39
APPASSIONATO	40
TO THE STATUE OF AN ARCADIAN SHEPHERD BOY	41
THALATTA	43
MY THRUSH	47
OH, HAPPY BROOKS	48
ÆOLUS	50
A DANCE OF THE DRYADS	52
BACCHANAL	55
SHADOWLAND	56
ASPIRATION	58
THE CATTLE COMING HOME	59

Contents.

	PAGE
TMOLUS	61
MARINERS OF THE WORLD	67
IL BEATO	68
LIKE THE LARK	77
AUTUMN	78
WIND ON THE SEA	82
MADRIGALS	84
O PALE COLD MOON	87
THE WILL-O'-THE-WISPS	88
THOR THE THUNDERER	91
THE VALKYRIER	93
SIEGFRIED'S SWORD	97
TITHONUS	99
WAKING	102
QUESTION	103
TAKE HER, KIND DEATH	104
SONNET—WITH A BUNCH OF ARBUTUS	105
SUMMER MIDNIGHT	106
AMONG THE MOUNTAINS	107
AN IDYL OF JUNE	110
MY LOVE IS LIKE THE DAWN OF DAY	113
CIRCUMSTANCE	114
THE FULNESS OF TIME	115
DANUBE BOAT-SONG	115
UNDINE'S FAREWELL TO HULDEBRAND	116
THE PARCÆ	118
A SYMPHONY OF THE HILLS	122
GO NOT, LONG SUMMER DAY	130
TO A ROSE CAST UPON A STREAM	131
MONADNOCK CROWNED	131

Contents.

	PAGE
Jetsam	133
Evensong	133
Progression	135
Vespers of the Hermits	136
Sattva	139
Fly, My Song	140
Night Piece	140
Upon a Romanza of Schumann	141
A Song for November	142
Never to Know	143
To-morrow and To-morrow and To-morrow	145
Like a Lute Touched by Facile Fingers	145
Transmutation	146
Swallows at Sunset	146
Going out with the Tide	148
Allegro Giojoso	150
A Song of Blossom	152
A Wind Rushed out of the Sea	153
The Lost Pleiad	155
Hymn to the Night	161
At Sunset	163
A Toast for the Year	165
Orpheus Sings	168
Rhapsody	176

Songs of Destiny.

"Give me truths,
For I am weary of the surfaces."
R. W. EMERSON.

I.

EARTH-TOUCH.

WE are but chaff, but chaff
   Swept on the wind—
Mocking storm-gusts that laugh,
   Whirling behind!
Poise have we none our own,
Axis and centre none,
Motes in a void alone,
   Gaugeless and blind!

We are but leaves, but leaves
   Wrenched from the tree,
Scattering fugitives
   No more to be;
Knowing not where we go,
Shrivelled and lying low,
Blotted by shroud of snow
   Impotently!

We are but breath, but breath
　　Breathed from a sigh,
Naught but a shibboleth
　　Swift to pass by;
Form is a shifting dream,
Substance too frail to seem
Aught but a transient gleam;—
　　Life all a lie!

Thus we disintegrate,
　　Crushed by the law?
Sport of a ruthless fate,
　　Cast on a shore
Strewn of all wreckages,
Chaos of that and this,
Where there no purpose is ;—
　　This—and no more?

Into the fecund earth
　　Falleth the seed,
Prescient of coming birth
　　Meet for its need.
Folded in darkling coil,
Warmed of the throbbing soil,
Steadfast thro' night's despoil
　　Till day succeed;

Earth-Touch.

Quick at its soul-sun's call
   Upward to thrust
Soft shoot through moldy pall;
   Cleaving the crust,
Drinking the sunshine there,
Basking in fervid air,
Building a being rare
   Out of the dust.

Thus of its vital need,
   Thus it achieves;
Breaking from rotting seed
   Burgeons to leaves;
Careth not what its power,
Whether of tree or flower,
Knows only 't is its hour
   And that it lives!

Casts by the outworn shell
   Now, nothing loth,
And by swift parallel
   Springs to new growth;
Changing the outward sign,
Guarding in secret shrine
Alway the germ divine,
   Life of them both.

Once in each musky copse
   Dwelt there a god,
Spirits on mountain tops,
   Souls in the clod.
Winds brought the whispered word,
And if a leaf but stirred
It was a god, half-heard,
   Mystery-shod.

Ah, in those ages old,
   Called pantheist,
Backward perspectives rolled
   Into the mist,
Simple men were of skill
And all untutored, still
Something they grasped at will
   Which we have missed.

Poisèd in Nature's arms,
   Made of her part,
Drained they life-yielding charms,
   Felt pulses start,—
Far-centred overflow,
Upsurging throe by throe,
Through all their vitals go,
   Warm from her heart.

Earth-Touch.

Child-like, she held them true
   Sons of her ken,
And the world's childhood knew
   Surelier then
How faith the world unlocks.
Here was no paradox;
Live were the rivers—rocks?
   Aye! *so were men!*

We of a later age,
   Sated, grown wise,
Come to our heritage
   Shorn of surprise.
Science the wonder shames;
Our artificial aims
Choke down the spirit-flames,
   Blot out the skies.

Blind in our vain conceit,
   May we command
One universe heart-beat?
   Wake with our hand
Star-glory, sunset flush?
Lay on the rose one blush?
Or yet as lark or thrush
   Praise understand?

Lo! every side a truth
   Plain to man's sight,
Spells of immortal youth
   Read but aright.
Everywhere miracle,
Nature's alembics full
Of new life wonderful—
   Secrets of light!

Still in thy bosom warm,
   Glad Mother Earth,
Keep'st thou the secret charm
   Of death and birth.
Winds bear the whispered word,
Breathes it through beast and bird,
And thy heart guards, deep-stirred,
   All we hold worth.

Stripped of our cumbrous wants,
   Thee will we woo,
Into thy sacred haunts
   Stealing anew,
Thy simpler ways to heed:
We are the seeking seed
Laid of our vital need
   On thy heart true.

Earth-Touch.

We of thine element
   All are made one;
Fashioned to like intent,
   Bared to same sun.
Swinging to natural law,
Equipoised more and more,
Soul-breaths with thee we draw
   In unison.

He who hath ears to hear
   Heed let him give,
He who hath soul for seer
   Let him perceive
Through thy sweet motherhood
One universal good,
One law, scarce understood,
   By which we live.

Pulses that come from thee,
   (Rock-throes or flowers,)
Bear all the mystery,
   Stir all the powers.
Out of the husk-born strife
Breaketh the god-head rife,—
Life, universal life!—
   Thy God and ours!

. . . . .

O sick and weary-wise,
   Once more return!
Underneath open skies
   Child-like grace learn;
Here waits the mystic shrine,
Lights unimpeded shine,
And in the grove divine
   Your altars burn.

II.

FIRE-BAPTISM.

DARE! Thou shalt be as a god,
    And the worlds be given thee;
At thy beck shall mountains nod,
Thou shalt put a yoke on the sea;
Unto thee be given—
So thou prove worth—
The keys of heaven
As well as earth.
The keys of the masterful occult powers
That hold all cosmic force in fee,
That leash the days and fetter the hours,
The talisman of supremacy;
If thou only fearless be,
If thou do but dare!
Art thou not more than the bird of the
    air?
The beast of the field, the worm in his root?
Fear is the meed of the brute,

The grosser reason that hath no hold
Of higher elements manifold,
So meets his cosmos mute.

But thou—thou art master.
And out of thy freedom greater
And out of thy tenure vaster—
Thine aspirations higher—
Thou shalt be judge and creator,
And thy thought shall purge as fire.
When pale fear rise—
The fleshly chill—
Thou shalt kill!
Thou shalt pierce through its sophistries
Till a shell it lies.
For thou *must* slay or be slain of it!
And Knowledge, the sanctifier,
And Courage, with torch star-lit,
Poised at the poles of life shall sit—
On the heights of understanding—
Arming the purpose that faints at naught,
The flame of endeavor heavenward caught,
And, ever expanding, expanding,
The circles dynamic of thought.

If I call to the deaf shall they hear?
If I sign to the blind shall they know?

Yet we are both blind and deaf in our fear,
Wrecking ourselves in the surface woe;
Knowing not whither we go,
Knowing not why we are here.
Yet we should know.
If we trace the steps below
We must surely see those above;
See the march of being move—
The higher out of the lower,
Each fulfilling its kind—
From the germ to the opened flower,
From the brute to the master-mind.
And beyond all the forces we know
There is force more imponderable,
More sublimated, more vital, more fine,
That shall breed a being more grand and full,
With never a severed line;
With never a break
'Twixt the far and near.
For the touch electric reaches us here
Straight from the astral sphere;
And all shall be ours to take.
Oh choose, and cease from the clod!
Oh spirit of man, awake,
Dare, and be as a god!

III.

STAR-MIST.

I DREAMED I was a beggar at the gate,
　　The beautiful gate wherethrough the busy throng
Poured morning, noon, and eve—flux and reflux—
Like some vast, surging sea;—some mighty tide
Now ebb and ebbing till with slimy tongues
The parched weeds lick the palpitating rocks,
Then flood and flooding with swift, briny breaths
Drawn from mid-ocean deeps, and sun-shot sparkles
Cleaving the emerald, as the shooting lights

Cleave and transfuse a gem; and evermore,
With sonorous, majestic mastery,
Rushing to fold the land in foaming arms!
From the still, dewy dawns, when roseately
The sun stole up and drowsed the morning stars,
Into the silver night sweeping the spheres
With the trailed glimmer of her dusky robes,
The great sea poured its never-ceasing flood,
But always left me stranded—and alone.
For I was one untoward fate had sealed
With vicious brand;—a vile, distorted thing,
Congenitally crippled; swept aside
From that far-surging sea whereon my soul
Would fain have sailed—a god-like argosy—
From port to port of fancy. Mine it was
To lie amid the loathing of my rags
And snuffle forth a cry for niggard alms;
And, if some passer-by more prodigal
Than others flung a ringing handful, fawn
In gratitude o'er-feignèd;—I who starved,

Starved for a food of higher elements!
I watched the evening star climb up and up—
A lambent beacon to the eyes of faith,
A symbol meaningless to me—then drew
My poor rags closer, crouched in grimmer mood
To lift my dumb reproaches till the dawn.
Alas! for days that pass and leave no sign,
Rolled in a calendar of vapors, swept
Like evanescent mists into the sea!
Dim dreams—half dreamed, chaotic, nebulous,
Tinged with a fringing light which never dawned—
Would vaguely stir me with an unnamed pang
To deeper wretchedness;—imaginings
Of some diviner world to be embodied
In harmony of form or tint or sound.
Thoughts crowded on me as a flock of swallows
Circle and vanish down a sunset sky.
I might have been a master artisan,
Fashioning dreams into fair stone, endued

With very gift of being; or, perchance,
Evoked from out the dull, unsensing wood
Rare visions, tinctured by th' enamelled wax
To exquisite conception; or, more free,
I might have measured all the empyrean
On the exalted wings of song. In me,
Dim and disordered, stirred the vital germ—
The central fire—which makes such visions live;
Only the gross flesh held me in its leash:
Only the flesh—the sordid, prisoning flesh—
Held me in leash! Know'st thou the wounded eagle,
A proud, strong thing, born to invade the heavens,
Dragged helpless by its malady to earth?
Its very impotence a ruthless goad,
It beats the traitrous air with frantic wings,
And chafes, and strains, and trembles back again
Broken and foiled. Oh, never, never yet
Have I put forth the power that in me lies!

Slain by its outward hurt, my spirit's wings
Battle with nothingness in passionate strife,
Only to break in dust and lie more prone.

And in a burning mist my dream went on.
Once, on a languid noon when the whole land
Lay in a semi-swoon of summer drouth,
And the hot beams crawled down the parching walls,
Pushing the narrowing shadow where, inert,
Lay man and beast in a dull mid-day drowse,
There came a mighty surge of trampling feet,
And babel tongues of clamoring multitudes;
And—as a sudden wind wakes answering voices
Through silent tree-tops, passing stir to stir—
There throbbed throughout the throng a murmurous cry,
"Jesus of Nazareth!" And others asked,
"Jesus of Nazareth who heals the sick?"

A sudden lull—as when a gusty pause
Palsies the breeze—held the vast horde in check.
I heard hoarse questionings and over all
One vibrant tone soared like a silver flute.
Less had a whirlwind moved me! Some wild power
Lifted my crippled frame; I clutched and tore
A bleeding passage 'mid the trampling feet—
Deaf to the cursing, blinded to the pain—
Until—withdrawn into a little space,
Hemmed and encircled by the stertorous crowd—
I looked upon him—him they called the Christ.
Not like a conqueror came he, armed and crowned;
Not in a hero's guise; but meanly robed
In bodily insignificance; yet still
About his brow there dreamed an astral mist,
As if he walked with angels and not men.
Serene he stood, a starry presence. Then
Nearer I crept, and with my wasted hands

Fingered his garments. Lightning-like he turned:
"What would'st thou?" and he dazed me with his glance.
"What would'st thou, friend?" "Lord, that I might be whole."
"Art thou *not* whole? The soul is always whole.
Behold!" Then leaning closelier he flamed
In mine the revelation of his eyes.

Strange, dusk-hued eyes wherein my spirit plunged
And lost itself, while the mad, cavilling world—
The sordid jostle and the empty noise—
Slipt from me like shed flakes. I seemed adrift
On some vast, inward, spirit-circled sea,
Unstirred by mutable wind or mortal tide,
Stretching from sight in fair beatitude—
A mystical transparency. Everywhere
There was a brooding glory like the day,
But more transcendent; yet I saw no sun,

I only knew its presence; and strange lights—
Dazzling prismatic tongues—transpierced the waters
To untold depths. Illimitable space
Throbbed with a luminous pulse, a coruscation
Of mingled flame and fluid;—now suffusion
Of myriad electric hues, now swept
Into a paling glamor, lustrously
Circling to wide affinities, outblotting
All time, all gauge, all concept of condition!
And every tiniest atom seemed alive—
One candent drop from some exhaustless fountain!
As in irradiate dawns fair lotus cups,
Folded and dewy, feel the breath of day,
And faintly, faintly, with a crucial throe,
Tremble to waking 'neath the summoning beam;
So with divinest tremors my soul woke;
And like a floating flower-cup I lay
Draining wide draughts of sempiternal truth.
And then meseemed this iridescent sea

Was the life-tide of spiritual perception.
The world which I had known was swept
    away;
I stepped within the vaster world of knowl-
    edge.
Creation is a myriad-fibred pulse
Drawing its flame-beats from one central
    fire,
One with it and indissoluble; so
In all things is the vital touch innate—
Worm or archangel; 't is the conscious
    sense
Of the immutable glory which makes life;
And soul is recognition.   Everywhere
The lower doth ascend from law to law,
In growths that brook no hindrance and
    no haste,
Vast-organized, unstaying. We who hold
Some glimmer of the Eternal, hold the keys
Of grander or of meaner, with our thought
Uplifting or debasing; — mind being
    winged,
And high thought spiritual presence
    realized.
Nor flesh sets bounds to sublimated flight;
These mortal manumissions men call death

Being but doors which ope to wider ranges.
Consists not life in spendthrift law of doing,
But the supremer one of being; rests
In the expanded orbits of the soul
Whose axis is the central solar core—
Is God himself !

One meteoric moment stood I thus,
For truth is flashed by single signal fires
When the initiate is ready; then—
Dissolving like the pageant of a dream—
The crowding, trampling human surge swept on,
Leaving but hollow echoings in ears
Held and attuned to finer cadences.
And was I healed ?   I never paused to ask.
No more I feel the temporary dress.
For me time is not, and those grosser webs—
Self-spun—which sometime seem to clog the sense
Are also melted like a sun-smit fog.
He who is made alive in heart is whole,
And hath nor claim nor question nor denial,
But rests—a god—in the eternal law,
Knowing his destiny.

IV.

DESTINY.

THERE is no death, no death! The veil is lifting,
  The veil is lifting from the mortal sight!
Dull fogs into Cimmerian deeps are drifting,
  Through premonitions of immortal light.

There is no death, no death! The great stars beckon
  Like fiery guide-marks through the dark to day;
We have our chart, the upward course we reckon,
  We cannot turn aside nor miss the way.

There is no death, no death! Through unknown places
  We voyage with a true, unswerving helm;
We sweep infinitudes of stellar spaces,
  Still aiming for some higher, vaster realm.

We know the measure of our aspiration
  Is founded in the measure of the law,
That cannot stay its own ordained creation,
  But must advance, advance forevermore,—

A seamless web; with ending and beginning
  Fixèd beyond the plenitudes of time,
And which the soul of man is ever spinning
  Into a comprehension more sublime.

We know the circles of increasing vision
  Shall probe in regions evermore supreme,
And shed the finite guises of transition
  As sleepers shed the vapors of a dream.

We know that change is but in man's per-
    ception
  Which metes all semblance by one little
      day,
Still faintly schooled into that fine concep-
    tion
  Of life which cannot ever pass away.

We know these fires of our inward yearning
  Which rend us with their purport, faint
      and dim,
Are sacred flames upon God's altars burn-
    ing;
  The quickening links which bind us
      unto Him,—

The immanent and all-pervading Presence,
  The one vast, throbbing pulse which
      moves the sphere,
The indestructible and vital Essence
  By which alone *we are*, both now and
      here.

     .   .   .   .   .   .

Hast thou not seen the summer midnight
    dreaming

On northern shores betwixt two mysteries,
From hemisphere to hemisphere still seeming
Reflected currents of opposing skies,

Whose flame-tongued surges, luminously blending,
　The shadowy confines of all things immerse,
Like a full, orbic tide—far-rolled—unending—
　To sweep the reaches of the universe?

Touched with a symboled aureole eternal,
　The great world lies in calm, transfigured might,
Surrendered to its syncope nocturnal,
　Surrendered to its miracle of light!

The west still tinctured with a lingering glamor,
　The waiting east suffused with kindling charms,
'Till swiftly, with a rapt, celestial tremor,
　The morning takes the evening in its arms!

Softly the gloaming melts, serene and tender,
　God-like the dawn-ray leaps, with flaming breath
That swells and floods into majestic splendor—
　Into the day!
　　　　THERE IS NO DEATH, NO DEATH!

Miscellaneous Poems.

MIRACLE.

IT is day!
    Over the mountain tips
The delicate stream
Of a color-dream
Wavers and flushes and slips;
The pinnacles all are agleam
As if they were swept by phantom lips.
Every somnolent hollow, void
With veils of night, hath decoyed
Some amber shaft of day;
Lurk as it may,
The darkness is ravished away!
The great crags laugh, and the little streams leap
Heedless and headlong adown the steep,
While the mist-wreaths upward and upward creep,
To melt evanished—sifted and shaken—
Life-overtaken.

Miracle.

The face of the dappled meadow
Folded in drowsy shadow
Still lieth, but oh! the finger of love
Shall over it move;
Its beauty with new grace invest,
And bid it awaken,
Awaken and joy with the rest!
Sunbeams acreep in the grass,
Sunbeams aflame in the sky,
Where great white cloud-pageants surging by
Snatch rose-tints as they pass!

The Earth is singing a song!
Long, long
She spins the winsome tune,
Like a mother's cradle-croon
To her infant ruddy and strong.
To her love the budding year
She sings in numbers clear,
And where no live things were
There passeth a stir;
The slumb'rous ones hear it and understand;
At the word of loving command
They haste to answer her.

Miracle.

For lyrics of Spring and Birth
Singeth our Earth.
Not a hillside so held in its wintry swoon,
Not a naked forest so sere and brown
But must feel a thrill of its power;
Not a calyx so folded down
But shall know its hour.
'T is as if a wizard's wand
Had circled on every hand,
Some chill enchantment had overthrown,
And liberated the land.
She is clothèd anew,
Our sweet Earth-Mother,
All fresh things vying with one another
Each to don a daintier hue!
One could scarce tell whether
The half-heard drift of the breeze
Harping alone through the trees,
Or those cloud-flakes so airily dressed,
Or the flash of color but half expressed
In yonder tall grass-feather,
Be the tenderest;—
All are so perfect together!

OF MY STAR.

THERE 'S a star that shines for me
   In the brooding firmament,
Past, present, and to be
   The goal of my heart's content.
Mine evening star in the dark,
   My morning star with the day,
She sheds through the heavenly arc
   Her soul's serenest ray.
And so high she burns, and true,—
   Where the lights celestial are,—
That she lifts me upward too
   With her love :—my star—my star!

O goal of my heart, my star!
   What matter if earth be cold,
And error attempt to mar
   Love's miracles manifold?
I shall neither fail nor faint,
   I doff the burden of care,
For she shields me from life's attaint,
   She fends from the world's despair.
And aye through the firmament,
   As the holy gates unbar,
I shall enter in and be blent
   With her love :—my star—my star!

APPASSIONATO.

PAOLO TO FRANCESCA.

OH! I will love thee with a love so strong
  That it shall breast the surge and bar the tide;
My spirit on its passion swept along
  Must cleave to thine though worlds on worlds divide.
I know no rest where thou dost not abide,
  Thine only touch my torn heart may restore;
Divinely perishing, unsatisfied,
  As life doth fleet forever more and more
    Still will I love thee!

Oh! I will love thee with a love so vast
  That it shall bridge o'er life and vanquish death;
The storm, the strain, the anguish overpast,
  The darkness of this night which openeth
To day, be as a flickered candle's breath.

The stars may fade, the universe past be,
Yet, borne on pinions of a tireless faith,
Across the threshold of eternity
    Still will I love thee!

TO THE STATUE OF AN ARCADIAN SHEPHERD BOY.

THOU blowest thy pipe on the lea,
    And thy tame sheep answer thy call;
The wind with its ungauged minstrelsy
Wafteth thine echoes o'er many a sea;
    But the sweetest of all
Is the song thou art breathing to me.

The song of a world ever young,
    Unpoisoned of greed or of heat,
An infant purity—long unsung,
A faultless grace from the fair earth wrung,
    Wind-wings for the feet,
And a pæan on every tongue.

In the jostling street's discord
    With its fetid atmospheres,
The strongest arm must aye be lord.

Though the sky be high and the earth be broad,
   'T is his fellows' tears
He heaps with his impotent hoard.

Away from the brutal stress—
   The false-dipping scale of the mart!
There is no gold in the flower's dress,
We may take of her treasure and leave none the less;
   To the unspoiled heart
The lowliest things will bless.

The forests no bargainings know,
   They spring not by custom or rule.
Would'st thou rise to thy man-god stature ?
     —then go—
Trust the Oreads—they will feed thee enow,
   In their worshipful school
Where the soul-wings have room to grow.

Lo! a presence peeped from yon wood,
   A star-smile flashed from the stream;
The voices call us from forest and flood;
In flutter of garments marvellous-hued,

They start from a dream,
And people the solitude.

Lives there no touch to read
  The hieroglyph of this lore?
Shall life's pageant pass and never take
      heed?
Must our world lie fallow and barren
      indeed
  For centuries more,
With its fruitless and slumbering seed?

Alas, for a grace long flown!
  Alas, for the silent flute!
I call to thee, but the echo's tone
Mocks me,—the accents are all mine own;
  And thou?—thou art mute,
Thou shepherd boy carved in stone!

THALATTA.

SLOW, slow,
    Over the sea,
Low, low,
    And mysteriously,

Eddied, purling,
Crisping, curling,
Over the shallows and seaweedy beach,
Down the dunes and the long sand-reach;
Sing thou a song to me!

A languourous dream
Of emerald deeps,
Where the wan sunbeam
Flickers and sleeps.
Grottoes gemmed
Amid phosphor seas,
Fringed and hemmed
With anemones.

Many a column
With nakre set;
High dome solemn,
Where waters fret.
A palace beautiful
Fit for a sea-king's rule;
With portals dusky-wet,
Weed-festooned and cool,
For a sea-king's vestibule.

Sing me a song of the restless main,
  Great waves heaving and whelmed and crossed;
The shrilling scream of the hurricane
  Over the drift of white foam tossed.
A song of courage that could not fail,
  Ploughing the wastes of a pathless track;
Of stout sails trimmed to the treacherous gale,
  Of ships that have sailed and never come back.
      Picture me too
      The valorous crew
That the swirl of the waves down-drew.

The ruthless effort, the pitiless strain
Of arms that battle the surge in vain;
Of flagging hands in their vice-like grip,
Dank with the salt and the death-sweat drip;
Of voices that call and are never heard;
Of hearts through the death-pang torn and stirred
  Only to send back one word!
      Flow, flow,
      Over them flow!

What do they know
Of the opaline caves below?

Warm, warm
Broods the summer calm.
Far and near
The sun burns clear
Through a lucent atmosphere.
Never a sigh
Of strife gone by
Comes re-echoing here.
Only an indolent sea-bird's cry,
A sea-bird's cry and a charmèd breeze
Hushing the deeps with its lullaby:—
These, only these.
But white waves waking,
Creeping, breaking
Each over each,
Pointing the beach
With feathery spume,
Dimpled and soft
Like an outworn plume
By sea-maid doffed;
Ever come speaking
The tale of a day,
Of a ship that sailed away.—
Ah me!—was it yesterday?

MY THRUSH.

AGAINST the burnished tint
Of saffron dreaming into opaline
Through western skies, with half a hint
Of evanescent green
Above them in a shimmering overglow;
Poisèd upon a long and leafless bough,
Seeming between heaven and earth to hang,
He swayed and sang.

He swayed and sang as if his tiny throat
Too fragile were to bear the ecstasy
Of such divine heart-flood,
Which through the solitude,
With every leaping note,
And every rhythmic trill,
The measure of the silence seemed to fill.

Ah! not for him
The creeping shadow and the cloistral gloom.
His spirit hath no room
For spectre dim,
For pain, or darkness, or despondency,
Or those strange pangs that lie

Deeper than tears, which to the voiceless come.
Far above all,
He, like a prophet pure and passional,
Fronting the illimitable flight
Of day amid trails of light,
Its promise seals, and through the empyrean
Breathes his high pæan:—
A psalm of aspiration and delight!

OH, HAPPY BROOKS!

OH, happy brooks that croon amid the wood,
  Or lightly loiter by some leafy dell,
Your voices are the songs of solitude,
  With limpid joy in every syllable,
And tender tremors in your quirls and crooks.—
    Oh, happy brooks!

The frail fern woos you, trailing through the wet,
  And fronds of crimson drink your overflow,

And star-eyed blossoms amid mosses set;
  While flights of sunbeams flicker as you go
To sleepy pools some gnarlèd tree o'erlooks.—
    Oh, happy brooks!

Dim dreams still greet us through the foliage.
  Balsamic whispers, lingering lone and late,
Tell of a sweeter and a simpler age—
  Revealed alone to the initiate—
Which all our artificial day rebukes.—
    Oh, happy brooks!

Perchance within some far-withdrawn retreat,
  Where dimpling ripple over green sedge slips,
The wild-wood nymphs have viewed their image sweet,
  Or shyly kissed you with immortal lips,
Then, startled, fled away to deeper nooks.—
    Oh, happy brooks!

Oh, happy brooks that in your bosoms
    bear
    The soul of Arcady, forever young!
You bring us all her joyance unaware;
    There is a living lyric on your tongue—
A wordless essence of unwritten books.—
    Oh, happy brooks!

ÆOLUS.

Heard ye my sigh
    Wakened mysteriously
Out of eternal space ?—
From the midnight's bosom deep,
From the arms of sleep,
Wafted it knoweth nor whence nor
    why;
Gift with the grace
Of celestial space;
Soft as unuttered note
That low in the fledgling's throat
Hovereth, hovereth;
Faint as a breath
Of roses as they die.—
Heard ye my sigh ?

Heard ye my song
Whispered the stars among?
I touched with my finger-tips
On the airy drifts of cloud
Till they laughed aloud
And swept my tender flutings along;
As a young thing sips
With eager lips
And joyance of heart and limb,
The goblet filled to the brim;—
The cup o'erfoamed and rife
With life, life, life,
With young life, sweet and strong!
Heard ye my song?

Heard ye my call?—
My herald of festival?
I swept off the early dew
From lilies in poolèd nook;
Drowsed buds I shook;
I leaped with the rainbowed waterfall;
And I loitered to woo
Where great fern-tufts grew;
I ruffled the silent lake,
And I bade the forests awake,—

Awake and follow, follow!
From holt to hollow,
Lo! I will gather them all!
Heard ye my call?

A DANCE OF THE DRYADS.

CHANT ROYAL.

DUSK on the terrace towers the dreaming pine,
  The chestnut slumbers up the craggy steeps,
The budding broom low-droops in drowsy line,
  The myrtle in the shadowy hollow sleeps.
The strong air, whence all life doth emanate
Forever, in quiescent mood doth wait,
And leaves the land wrapped in ethereal trance;—
Not one untuneful note nor dissonance
  To steal a glamour from the perfect night,

While down the mossy coverts we advance.—
  'T is good to taste the measure of delight!

Bind garlands; dill with violet combine,
  Woven with cassia and wind-flower that weeps.
Around our brows wreathe the lush, trailing vine,
  Through whose dark folds the ripening cluster peeps.
Across the greensward fair nymphs, hasting late,
Shall scatter buds and blossoms delicate,
So that, amid the glittering expanse,
Wherever foot shall fleet or vision glance
  The fragrant flood the spirit shall invite,
And the sense feast on rich luxuriance.—
  'T is good to taste the measure of delight!

Hold the hands fast,—the fond clasp intertwine,
  As up the seven-voiced pipe the music creeps;

And, when the wingèd lyre shall give the sign,
  Let loose the fetters of young blood that leaps!
Lithe forms shall twirl and tremble, mate to mate,
And young lips make the silence passionate
With the glad life that springs for utterance.
No laggard step, no fret nor dalliance
  To stay the rapture of the midnight's flight,
Love leadeth and immortal is the dance.—
  'T is good to taste the measure of delight!

O Golden Artemis, upon us shine
  The livelong hours! Where thy pure radiance sweeps,
The world is made mysteriously divine,
  And living wonder lurks in hidden deeps.
Dionysos crown we in his regal state
With vine and fruit, and hail him king, elate;

And purple-stainèd Pan, whose haunts we chance.
Above them all thy glorious countenance
  Reigneth supreme—a universe alight:
Make thy supernal kiss our heritance.—
  'T is good to taste the measure of delight!

BACCHANAL.

RAISE on high the cup,
    Pour the fiery wine,
  Ruby, frothed, and fine;
    Fill it up!
Lo! how dance the sparkles in the light,
  Shot with kisses from the burning sun;
Lo! how bubbles foam and break from sight,
    O'er the beaker's brink,
And adown the flagon over-run.
    Drink the perfect wine!
    Drink the gift divine!
      Drink!

    Drain the draught again;
    Fire unconfine;

  Mark with burning sign
   Heart and brain!
Through the sources floods the flaming
   throe,
 Every thew and sinew waxing strong;
And the wingèd spirit 'neath the glow
   All forgets to think,
 Leaping upward in spontaneous song.
   Drink the perfect wine!
   Drink the gift divine!
    Drink!

SHADOWLAND.

BACKWARD and forward the shadows go
 Over this veil which we call life,
Shifting and drifting to and fro,
Spun in a vague and vanishing show;—
 Shadow and shimmer rife.

Greeting, they pass in the fluctuant drift;
 Drifting, they meet and greet and are gone,
Some with the seeming touch of a gift,
Some undefined, as the low mists sift,
 Some like a sigh forlorn.

What are they seeking and what do they
    bring?
  What do they do with that thing called
    life?
Lift they it up for an offering?
Sink it in slough as an animal thing?
  Crush it with low-born strife?

One swift turn of the whirring wheel,
  One short turn of the wheel of Time;
Out the figures familiar reel,
New shapes into the pageant steal;—
  Puppets in pantomime!

What doth it matter if tear or smile
  Paint the hour that fleets away?
We too—we—in a little while
Out of the vapors shall silent file
  Into the yesterday.

What hast thou found in that shadowland—
  Knowledge-mongering egotist?
Hast thou a grasp of a spectral hand?
Hast thou a foothold on which to stand—
  Thou shadow out of a mist?

ASPIRATION.

FADE world, and leave me free!
 Fade sense!
So that the meanings of Omnipotence
Burn clear in me.

Like infants' murmurings
 Pass strife!
 Thou dost not touch the central core of
  life,
But fleeting things.

O'er circumstance and time
 Sweep soul!
 And know them vapors which have no
  control
Of things sublime.

Why, like a homeless waif
 Forlorn,
 Should I against each gross, low-lying
  thorn
My spirit chafe?

Why, like a driven leaf,
 Wind-thrust,

Toss aimless with each momentary
    gust,—
My clasp as brief?

Pavilioned over all,
  Star-fed,
  The Heaven of eternal thought is spread.
Therein, withal,

My hungered soul may fare,
  And draw
  The life-elixir of that higher law,
And blossom there.

THE CATTLE COMING HOME.

ALL Ipswich marshes lie ashine,
    Held in the flame-trance of the sun
That burns the west to panoplies
Of gold and crimson, pearl and dun.
Wan vapors wreathe the misty line
Of hills that link the land cross-wise;
While through the nearer marshlands run
The tidal rillets, serpentine
And sluggish, with half-opened eyes;
And all the emblazonment of skies
    In them reflected lies.

The Cattle Coming Home.

All living nature seemeth dumb,
The land enwrapt in endless still,
And bird and insect silent, till
A tender wind begins to blow
    From the remotest hill.
And fitfully the echoes grow
Of footfalls faint that nearer come;
And, now and then, breathes soft the low
Of the cattle coming home.

Footfalls that greaten and grow clear
Across the twilit meadows far,
Till through the dusk the horns — spread
    wide—
Of Black Bess come, and then the star
Of Silverhead, and they are here!
In laggard ranks, half side by side,
Half trailed in lines dissimilar
That break and join and interfere,
Of bovine dullness occupied,
They push where marsh and creek divide,
    And tramp the painted tide.

They stamp amid the gleaming loam,
And break my pictures beautiful;
And up the wet stalks, dark and cool,

They scatter glories through the grass
    From each prismatic pool.
But now the sweet lights fade and pass,
To leave the land in monochrome;—
I only catch the moving mass
Of the cattle coming home.

TMOLUS.

OUT came he from his forest fastnesses,
    From mossy grottoes where naiads bathe and drink;
For the hidden haunt of the timid stag is his,
    And the lair of the bear and the skulking wolf and mink.

Up through the palpitant air his tawny mountains
    Cleave like a frozen billow, wave on wave,
Wet with the ceaseless tears of an hundred fountains,
Torn with inward throes into chasm and cave.

Now were the naked crests flushed saffron and pink,
   Touched by the finger-tips of the goddess Aurora,
As, up and down, to the very precipice brink,
   The fearless feet of her airy chargers bore her.

Still down the valley's flanks the forest slumbered,
   Purples and shimmering grays and melting blues,
Where—hoary shafts erect, a host unnumbered—
   The great trees ranged in endless avenues.

And ever back and forth hung the mountain mist,
   Webbed through the leaves, a pale, diaphanous thread,
Till caught in the rosy arms of the dawn and kissed,
   And who shall say where it turned and vanishèd?

Tmolus.

Stumbling out of his deeps came the great god Tmolus,
  Rugged and stern and shorn of tenderness;
For the dawn's enticements he cared not a flat obolus,
  And he shaded his shaggy brows from the wind's caress.

He blew out the cups of the flowers that dance and glisten,
  He swept the forests aside with a turn of his shoulder,
He folded his hirsute arms and paused to listen
  On the barren crest of a tempest-ravened boulder.

Over against, on a crag, sat the great god Pan,
  To his mouth his belt of reeds, close-bound and hollow;
And near, on a rose-tipped cloud, in the image of man,
  With his stringèd shell in his hand, lay Phœbus Apollo.

The matted locks of the great Pan did eclipse
  The little horns that above his temples grew,
As he raised the syrinx up to his eager lips,
  And a challenge smiled to the world as he softly blew.

Out of the seven-voiced pipe came Earth's sweet stress;
  The wood-dove's amorous plaint, and the tender coil
Of blossoms shyly oped to the sun's caress,
  The very throe of the seed in the germinant soil.

Over the lands went the wood-wild summons voicing;
  Little brooks laughed and a smile swept over the seas,
And the hill-tops echoed the strain with swift rejoicing,
  For never were heard such ravishing sounds as these!

Then the other attuned his lyre, and, preluding
  With fitful cadence and dissevered chord,
Touched idle fingers over the vibrant string;
  Then into a lofty rapture swept and soared.

Fraught with ecstasy, thrilling with passionate pain,
  Life and Love incarnate seemed to spring,
As up and up swelled the strong, compelling strain,
  And set the heart of the universe answering.

Great gnarlèd forest trees rocked, line on line,
  Delicate flowers sprang up from the emerald sod,
And ferns reached forth, each on its quivering spine,
  As all of them turned their heads and faced the god.

Wild creatures, one by one, each from his lair,
  The summons breathed in the searching theme obeyed;
The little fawn came down with the savage bear,
  And the wood-squirrel with the serpent, unafraid;

While out from the forest glooms and the broken rocks,
  With many a twitter and chirp and twirl and twire,
All feathered things swept down in rushing flocks,
  And hung like a cloud above the god and his lyre!

Then, with a thunderous cry from his high retreat,
  Down did the mighty Tmolus madly spring,
And flung his ponderous bulk at Apollo's feet;—
  "Lo! thou hast borne me a soul; art thou not king?"

MARINERS OF THE WORLD.

MARINERS of the world,
   Whither, whither steer you?
Your sails so swift unfurled
By fitful winds are whirled,
The treacherous shoals are near you.
Nor gauge nor guide the great main hath,
The void no almanac,
How plough the wastes without a path?
How know the shifting track?
How shall the distant port be won—
The harbor of the sun?

Mariners of the world,
Whither, whither speed you?
With surges tossed and curled
Some soaring beacon need you.
Stout of limb,
What may force avail you?
Skies grow dim,
Oar and silk sail fail you.
Trust not your souls to the bending spars;
Steer by the stars,
Mariners of the World!

IL BEATO.

A meditation of the painter, Benozzo Gozzoli, upon the death of his master, Fra Giovanni Angelico da Fiesole.

HE is gone—the master—him I have served so long,
  My star from the shining firmament hath set!
No more through the matins I hear celestial song,
  For earth unto earth hath repaid her mortal debt,
Freeing the soul to blossom to endless light;
It is I alone who am left in the void and night.

Il Beato, men called him—the blessèd—but which of them knew
  The whole intent of his holy and high desire?
For the purified vision is given only a few
  To see through the veiling flesh to the altar fire

Streaming upward and upward in flame
   divine,
Making the human heart as a temple
   shrine.

God wot he might portray Heaven! Nearer
   to him
  Was the atmosphere of that high society
Than the cloisters he dwelt amongst, and
   the cherubim
  Swept him alway with their wings and
   kept him free
From the sordid touch of the world's con-
   tinual jar,
Till his sanctified spirit greatened into a
   star.

He could rest tranquil where lesser men
   importune,
  He never strove for his vision; prayer-
   ful and dumb,
He waited the word of his Lord in rapt
   commune,
  Knowing surely the summoning call
   would come.

Then he would rise and toil, and his love was such
The very colors glowed deeper beneath his touch.

Impotent mortar waxed to a sentient grace,
  And tenderest life awoke from the senseless panel,
The praise in his heart shining out of each saintly face
  As if of itself,—his hand the unconscious channel
Of that tide of inspiration which might flow
Through all men's veins if all were but pure enow.

Instinct with passion, fresco and triptich grew warm,
  Like a glittering weapon drawn from the shrouding sheath;
But those who only see the color and form
  Miss the finer truth of the meaning underneath;
A truth immeasurably mystic, sweet and choice—
Too elusive for speech, which only music might voice.

For color and form be but the elements,
  The cosmic forces, that pass through the crucible
Of the poet's fiery thought, to issue thence
  Transmuted into a power of finer spell
Than merely the lineaments of beauty and youth,
To breathe through the ages immortal love and truth.

I sometimes think that he never saw the world
  At all, but dwelt serene on the mountain tops.
For him over noisome fens drifted vapors pearled,
  And only light filled the dark, ensanguined copse,
While the sunset held alway a vision of angels' wings
To his rarefied sight, so lifted in highest things.

The world in its feverish strife—athirst, adust—
  Hath need of a few winged souls from its weary level

To rise and sow broadcast the seeds of a trust
  Too crowded with grace to harbor a cleft for devil.
Though they walk 'midst their fellow-men unsceptred, unseen,
The ground is holy wherever such souls have been.

So dwelt the master—of us, yet not of us;
  A lamp in the portal, a star in the infinite arc,
Shining in fixèd faith unswervingly—thus—
  Whether men paused to see or passed in the dark.
The few who gathered around him to pencil and paint
Caught, as he touched us, the aureole of the saint.

The many beheld in him only a dreamer of dreams;
  A unit—apart—in a self-colored world all ideal;
But which of us all can swear that the thing as it seems

Through the shifting report of the recusant sense is the real?
The impact external—self-centred, self-serving, confined—
Or the outpouring shaft of light from the luminous mind

That knoweth existence can only be such as we seek
Or make with the thought of its governance? 'T will be the brute,
If the mind look for brutishness only; let the soul speak,
And, under the rule of love made absolute,
Life would spread out like a deep, translucent pool
Mirroring Heaven, awesome and beautiful.

Ah, methinks that the strain of spirit forever high-fixed
Must sharpen away the links of this bodily chain
To slenderest threads; for we live two worlds betwixt,
And though the higher must still of the less be fain

A lingering while, the veil is so thin—so
    thin—
The hallowed thought *might* lift it and
    glance within.

God is a spirit; they who would worship
    Him
  Must come in the spirit's wedding gar-
    ment drest;
Purified, purged of the personal rags that
    dim
  Hearing and sight from the union mani-
    fest:—
Uttermost self-surrender, passionless, still,
Volition absorbed in the one Supernal Will!

At one—at one!—one with the causal
    whole;
  The circle perfect, rounded on every
    side!
Then indeed through the open gates of the
    soul
  The gaugeless truth would rush in a
    rapturous tide;
And God revealèd be with never a bar,
Life of lowliest atom or loftiest star!

Their very essence and being—all that is:
　The outward semblance being the en-
　　velope,
The beautiful vesture of God, in genesis:—
　Sun-vapors over the Hills of Eternal
　　Hope
Drifting to law of sequence transitory
Till vision grow strong enough for the un-
　　veiled glory.

God is a spirit; we of His handicraft,
　Gendered of Him, are we not spirit too?
And where in immortal should ever the
　　mortal shaft
　Of passion or pain find a weakness to
　　welter through
Save in the thought of wrong? If the
　　thought be light,
The beacon is up and the way is clear
　　through the night.

And the Reaper grim, what should he
　　claim of us
　Save the robe we want no more and
　　would lay aside

For other covering—larger, more luminous—
  Lest the shell the spirit's expanding grandeur hide?
Grudge him not shadows: starveling he is at last,
For we pass not away, but only seem to have passed.

Oh, rest not foiled in the sense of a pigmy stature,
  Lost in atmospheres of mutable earth!
Rather rise to the grasp of our puissant nature,—
  Children of Light that we be—and know our worth;
Know we might be as Gods so we *dared* to be,
And over evil and death hold the mastery.

Joy, for the hope immortal, now and here!
  Joy, for quickening power, never stayed!
Though prisoned still with the gyves of self and fear,
  Though the seal of my liberty be long delayed,

I have lifted a tithe of the veil for a dazzled glance,
And I know the Truth that is neither dream nor chance.

Did I say he had died—my master? Ah no, no death
  On growth so perfect could lay its finite part,
And he who hath alway breathed the heavenly breath
  Could only rise more high for the flame in the heart;
If I seem to have lost him 't is only that sight is too dim,
Too fearful, too stultified still to follow him.

LIKE THE LARK.

LIKE the lark, like the lark
    Cleaving the heavenly arc,
On quivering wings rejoicing,
A vision of sunrise voicing,
And flinging his message o'er open and cloud
Till the very winds sing aloud,

In the spell of his rapture caught:—
So uprises my thought.

The song of the lark must end
And the singer descend.
Weary at last in his flight,
The pæan hushed and the sweet throat dumb,
Sorrowful, shorn of delight,
He must sink—sink—sink and alight;
Back to earth he must come.

But my thought, but my thought
Abideth, returning not.
For oh! through the æther rare
It hath soared and trembled and drifted,—
Drifted all unaware
Through the shining gates uplifted,
And hath found its harbor there:—
For my thought is a prayer.

AUTUMN.

NOW come the days when life awhile stands still,
And, wrapped in temperate contemplation, views

All that shall be and was; with opened eyes
Reads presage in what seemed but darkened text
Writ cross-grained on the pages of the past,
And, mirrored in the future, dimly sees
The promise perfected;—so dares to pause
And let the calm peace fill and be fulfilled.
Thus Nature pauses too and lets the year—
Her finite guise—put on ephemeral hues,
And pander sense to sense, and pass away,
The semblance of its brief day being o'er,
Robed in the fitting splendors of decay.
Past is the travail of birth and tender growth,
The pang of blossoms waste by early storms,
Of fruitful buds made cripple and distort
By unsought frosts. Past is the summer's glut
Of rounded branch and perfect foliage.
The fierce noon-heat hath bred the tempest-gust
And the destroying whirlwind, which have torn

Filament from filament, scorched with
    searching fires
The springs of being. Only all these throes
Are overpast, forgotten, swallowed up
Beneath that healing touch of joy which
    links
Finite with infinite; and so to-day
Nature doth lend to sense her inward
    grace.

Lo! up the steeps of trending hillsides,
    wrapped
In sombre mantle of the conifers,
Now here, now there, like flocks of flame
    burst forth
The conflagrations of the maples, each
Flaunting to each a more o'erwhelming
    glow.
Over the gray, hoar rocks the mercury
Rushes in scarlet fires, and leans to wreathe
The white and purple asters, and to mix
Its gleams amid the many-feathered weeds.
By every lonely pool the gentian lifts
Her modest head in eloquent loveliness;
While here and there some long-spared
    goldenrod

Autumn.

Still nods and strives to glean an aftermath
Of sunshine. Russet stand the seeded ferns,
And brown and burnt the nut-trees; every hour
Opens a little more the shrouding burr
Until some wind in idle sport shall pass
To shake the laughing harvest to the ground.
And, last of all the maskers lingering
At this prolongèd feast, the solemn oaks
Wait in their bronze and purple draperies,
Whose tints through pearlèd distances do melt
In a chromatic scale of color,—wait
To see the year a little older; then
By one and one, by leaf and twig and branch,
They doff and gently rustle to their feet
The useless garments they shall need no more.

Why should we shrink where Nature never shrinks?
Why should we not take heart of her whose heart

Enfolds the germ of all things?—dare to stand
With spirits bared before the ineffable light,
As she against the glory of the dawn
Lifts naked arms, all-welcoming the day?
And then, with her, lie down in quiet trust,
A sweet, brief space, beneath the coverlet
Of the warm purifying snows, and sleep
The peace of these waste senses' parting dream,
A wondrous sleep that doth awake in spring.

WIND ON THE SEA.

WHIP me my chargers—my chargers
    that wait in the bay!
For sluggard are they
With the heats of the day.
They are lying nose-deep in the cooling brine,
Snuffing the saltness up like wine,
Held of the drowsy drink supine.
Never a shake of the shaggy mane,
Never a toss of the tail again,

Never a white hoof lifted plain,
Never a ripple of spray;
Only a low, slow, indolent side
Heaving at ease on the mid-summer tide,
While the Nereids wait to ride.

Whip me my chargers! Deal them a mid-sea blow,
Scourge them, and lo!
A flicker of snow,
Of opal, of amber, of aquamarine,
The amethyst's flush and the emerald's green,
With deep, dark indigoes blended between.
For never was gem of such irised glow
As my chargers' lifted breasts
When they heave their shoulders and shake their crests,
And turn at the winds' behests.
Curbless, riderless, wild, and free
As the tempest-mothers whose foals they be,
Like heralds of equinox,
They rear themselves from the undulant sea,
Break and unite in a reckless dance

Each over each, with their manes askance,
Combing the blue in their swift advance;
And where harbor with land inlocks,
Fierce with the pulse of the savage north,
Nostrils hissing, inflamed and wroth,
White flanks laved of the churnèd froth,
They leap foam-mouthed on the rocks!

MADRIGALS.

I.

BEAR her my love, sweet flowers,—my very love
Of loves! For, through life's noon-day toil and heat,
My steadfast heart hath lain beneath her feet
Unnoticed. And perchance thy worth may prove
My heart's prayer, with her image interwove.
Bear her these kisses that I press on thee;
She will not know I kissed thee, so maybe
Against her own dear cheek thou mayst be pressed;

And call those tremulous dews upon thy
    breast
Mine unshed tears for her long cruelty.

II.

Oh! the sweet glamor of her presence!
    glance,
And touch, and tones of voice, and whim-
    sied arts
Too numberless for speech, that snare all
    hearts
Forever! I seem living in a trance
That hears her voice in every breeze, and
    plants
Her image on all objects, pure and sweet.
Ah! were I lying low, my race complete,
And over where I slumbered she should pass,
Methinks that as her footsteps crushed the
    grass
My very dust must rise and kiss her feet!

III.

Dear, though I do not hear thy loving
    speech,
Nor see thy heart within those fond eyes
    shine,

Deeper than time or separation reach
I feel thy love inevitably mine.
My compline and my matin prayer are thine,—
Thine image veiling every servile thing;
Thou livest in my heart as in a shrine
Where my most secret thought comes worshipping.

IV.

To know love *is* bringeth the full content.
Those outward things—contact and sight and speech—
Though they be rapture's self, can scarcely teach
A deeper meaning unto love's consent;
They are to knowledge but the complement.
O Sweet, we hold those outward symbols less
Than that deep consciousness of inward stress,
And love asks little of the perfect love.
So silence falling doth in essence prove
The soul's profoundest union,—fathomless!

O PALE COLD MOON.

O PALE cold Moon,
  With shadowy, ever half-averted face;
Chill at the core where fires should be bright;
Sweeping inanimate through soundless space,
Thou seemest but a spectre of the night—
An astral vision of long-fled delight—
A passion spent too soon!
Tell me, against thy silent heart doth beat
No lingering note from out the melody
Of that celestial tune
Thou once went singing in thy round complete?
Some echo from the spheral choirs to cheat
Time of its vast stagnation? Or hast thou,
Hast thou too tasted of that numbing air
Which rives all joy of power to quicken, saps
Cinereous sense of sympathy, and snaps
The live, tense, thrilling cords; so leaving thee,
Hardened and dimmed, a burned-out entity,

Down through the empty spaces of despair
Emptily whirling?

O Moon, the mantle of thy silver zone
Wraps all a glamored world with phantom
    charm
Of frosty glory which can never warm
One single germ to being; no, not one.
On me, too, lies a superficial light,
The paled reflection of diviner things,
But underneath the ash with cinder clings,
A colophon of blight.
Moon, in thy hollow pageant thou art not
    alone!

THE WILL-O'-THE-WISPS.

TRIP, trip,
   Slip, slip,
Like a spark
Where the dark
Beds of ooze
Lines confuse
With their gases!
Forms surprising,
Swift uprising,

  Rend the vapors
  With their capers.
  Open pinions!—
  We are minions
  Of morasses.
  Flitter, flutter;
  Nothing utter;
  Dumb, dumb;
  Turn and twist
  With the mist,
  Through the masses
  Of dank grasses.—
  Lo! we come, we come!

Through the ditches and the fosses,
If a soul our pathway crosses,
  Woe to him, woe to him!
Nerves shall falter, eyes grow dim,
And the vigor from its sources
  Shall depart each limb.
In confusion, in delusion
Nothing seeing, nothing heeding
He must follow all our leading.
  Now surround him,
  Swift confound him,
Daze him, craze him, sore amaze him,

  All his senses chain!
Then advancing, dancing, glancing,
Turning, shooting, convoluting,
  Leap again—again!
So bewilder and deceive him;
Then we 'll leave him, then we 'll leave him
  To his vain imaginings.
Thus we treat unwary mortals
That dare venture through our portals:—
  We are tricksy things!

    Now to cover!
    Sport is over,
    Over is our holiday.
    No remaining,
    Night is waning,
    So, complaining,
    We must hurry,
    Worry, flurry,
    Swift to hide our play.
    Scour the ledges!
    Sweep the sedges—
    Marsh and meadow;—
    Into shadow
    Hie away!

Flutter, flicker
Quicker, quicker!
Day is waking,
Dawn is breaking,
Overtaking
Every star.
Faint, far,
Fade from sight;
Quite, quite
Into night.
Out light!—
Vanishèd we are!

THOR THE THUNDERER.

OUT of the North thou comest,
    Thor the Thunderer!
Robed in thy cosmic majesty,
    Thor the Thunderer!
The winds from unknown voids
Shall fillet thy brow;
The polar hurricane
Whirl in thy hair;
And, gemming the belt of thy power,
As a zone of jewels resplendent,

The fulminant clouds encincture thee.
The heavens furnish thy throne,
The mountains thy footstool be;
As thou comest, insolent, haughty,
To claim thine own.
Thou shalt sport with the spheral Earth,
The labor of cycles shake;—
Toss the Earth as an infant's toy,
And she shall tremble before thee.
In her darkest caverns
The griping throe of fear shall pass,
The moan of travail be heard.
The deeps shall shudder and heave,
Shall shrink with a prescient dread
At thy touch, O Master of Terrors!
As when from lairs remote
In the thorny wildernesses,
The monarch of beasts,
The mighty lion, arousing,
Leaps superb from his covert;
And shaking the mat of his shaggy mane,
And lifting his tawny muzzle on high,
Flings over river and forest
His resonant, menacing challenge;
Every stricken creature that hears,
Turning from sleep or carousal,

Dripping the fear-born sweat from its
    flanks,
Mouthing delirious foam, —
Fleeth, fleeth
In panic it knoweth not whither;
So tremble the æons before thee,
So cowers the Earth at thy feet,
Thor the Thunderer!

THE VALKYRIER.

HEAREST thou not the maidens rush-
    ing—rushing—
  Swift through the shadowy night,
The rythmic tread of their plunging
    chargers crushing
  The clouds in headlong flight?

Fair are they, of a passing fairness seem-
    ing,
  With starry eyes that blind;
The loosened bands of their shining tresses
    streaming
  In the wind which whirls behind.

Strong are they, large-limbed and lithe and supple,
  With coursers fierce and tense;
The twain of them a grand and terrible couple
  Hurled through the elements.

Daughters of Asgard, bathed in immortal fire,
  Forms of power and grace,
Immortally they ride with a god-like ire
  Aflame in each upturned face.

Oh! they must ride and ride and naught disturb them;
  Nor starry deeps profound,
Nor wastes of space nor the whirlwind's onslaught curb them
  As they haste to the fatal ground.

Theirs the task 'mid the savage stress of battle,
  When the valorous arm shall fail;
When the trusty broadsword snaps and the mace-blows rattle
  On shivering links of mail;

Through hideous labyrinths, with death-
    blood reeking
  Of perished man and horse,
To pass with unscathed footsteps, seeking
    —seeking
  The hero's stiffening corse.

All silent they uplift, the prone form
    placing
  On the chafing charger's back;
Then away, away!—again to their furious
    racing
  Up the heaven's pathless track.

For aye, within the portals of Valhalla,
  He who is nobly slain,
Fallen as brave men fall in deeds of valor,
  In glory lives again.

Odin's own shall he be, his favors tasting,
  Fruits of fire and sword,
And shall sit in well-earned leisure grandly
    feasting
  At the Gods' exhaustless board.

And the maidens serve. From many a
    regal flagon,
  In cups of dazzling ore,

All weirdly wrought with scroll and rune and dragon,
  The foaming mead they pour.

So evermore with sound of mighty wassail
  The lofty roof-trees ring,
Where the great Gods sit with every hero vassal,
  Supremely banqueting.

    . . . . . .

When through the northern skies the burnished arrows
  Of boreal archers shoot
In a scintillant arc that swells and dips and narrows,
  With streamers revolute;

And there falls a strange, unearthly throb and crackle
  Through crisping air and frore,
An echo of fiery steeds and the hurtling tackle
  Of men at deadly war;

Know 't is the Valkyr maidens swift advancing
  Again up their ancient track,

And the weapons of heroes, glorified, and
    glancing
O'er a charmèd zodiac.

SIEGFRIED'S SWORD.

MASTERFUL gods have made decree
    Whoso striveth invincibly
Semi-god with themselves shall be;

Whoso stands through the nether strife
Forging himself in the darkness rife
Graspeth the talisman of life!

Fierce I forge through the night and dark,
Lurid leap of the anvil'd spark
Lifting the cavern's tenebrous arc.

Out of the gloom and grime and smutch
Springeth the glory that steads so much,
Clod transmute at a master-touch.

Blows but smite to unite the whole;
There, a breath of the living coal,
Here, the rivets which bind the soul.

Siegfried's Sword.

Men may pass in a world outside,
Light lips scoffing unsatisfied,
Here by the fiery forge I bide

Wrestling, sole, where no others know;
Stern, invincible, blow by blow
Forging the brute world's overthrow.

Every clang of the weltering steel,
Every stroke on the blade I deal
Marks a throe of the inward weal.

This for the high thought held apart;
This for a nature that beggars art;
This for the sign of a stainless heart;

This for courage that knows no flinch;
This for endurance, inch by inch;
This for calm at the final clinch.

Out of my solitude, gloom, and grime
Forge I the tool of a dream sublime,
Forge I the sword that shall vanquish Time.

Poignant, flexible, flame-endued,
See it flash from its sheathing rude—
Flash in the hand that knows it good—

Hot from the spirit's armories;
Fruit of my heart, of my handcraft, this
Greater than Thor with his hammer is!

Systems shall fall—a universe rock;
This shall cleave through the cyclic shock
Bringing to all things their Ragnerok.

Spelled am I in immutable youth,
Girt with the weapon of god-like sooth:—
Lo! the sword I have forged is Truth!

TITHONUS.

AN AUTUMN ODE.

ALAS, Tithonus!
    What dost thou here where all the
        world is dead,
And all the summer pæans have passed
        away,
And through the clouding day
The singers upon south-bound wings have
        fled:—
What dost thou here?
Lo! all the earth is naked, bald and sere.

In covert damps that bear the wood-beasts print
The star-weed withers with the fragrant mint;
And on the gusty breeze
Pale, downy seed-wings scud to farther' leas.
One single reedy head
Stands like a rattling phantom at the gate
Of summer, where the sweet days lingered late.
A frosty vapor veils the shining hills,
And all the solitary lowland chills.
From far away there steals a shivering breath,
A single note of sorrow unforgot,
A still, pervasive, brooding hint of death:—
But thou—thou heedest not.

Thou heedest not, Tithonus! All too soon
The frore spear pierceth through thy summer sheath;
Upon the faded sward thou liest prone.
And who shall count the wealth that thou hast known
Of glutted golden hours, so full, so full

Of the rich shows of life—fleet, beautiful?
So full of idle sport and idler song,
So crowded with delights the whole day
    long
Thou couldst not dream of ending, no, nor
    think
Life kept a hemlock draught for thee to
    drink;
Nor yet divine—this frozen midnight o'er—
Earth should awake once more.

And we, Tithonus,
What have we, vagrants, more than thou
    to show
For all the plenitude of summer's glow?
What have we garnered from our golden
    prime
Of that potential promise which low-lies
Beneath the song and dance and all which
    dies,—
That flowering of the spirit, sweet and
    wise?
Have we not lived, like thee, a transient
    hour
Creatures of chance and ignorant of our
    dower,

So that when Autumn turns her sombre page
We have no guerdon but the pains of age?
Ah me, Tithonus!
Are we not also Prodigals of Time?

WAKING.

IT is as if my soul had slumbering lain
   A senseless cumbrance; as, wrapped in strange calm,
In ancient crypts those little seeds of grain
   For æons have slept in duskiness and balm.
Yet when men feed them to the fecund soil
They burst at once in leaf and bud and coil.

None dream the years they lay quiescent there;
   Kingdoms have crumbled since they fell asleep,
Awaiting for the single breath of air,
   The single fervid touch of sun, to leap
From death-trance in a long-forgotten tomb
Into a living joy of leaf and bloom.

And I have wakened. Oh! I cannot know
  Whether my soul shall bear or bud or
    flower;
I only feel the surging life-blood flow,
  I only live my joy from hour to hour.
It is enough the sun hath breathed to rive
My slumb'rous death, and that I am alive!

QUESTION.

HOW does my soul know God? How,
  'neath the roof
  O'er wintry waters cast,
Do torpid creatures that wait in the frozen
    cloof
  Know that the sun hath passed
Unseen its vernal line? And suddenly
  River and silent pool
Are overflowing, like whirlèd sands in the
    sea,
  With new life wonderful.

How does my soul know God? How
    does the moth
  Feel a tremble of power,

Folded close in its dusky cocoon cloth;
  Know its appointed hour,
And somehow—somehow—wrestling film by film,—
  Loosing them every one,
Break ecstatic into the daylight's realm,—
  Into the fostering sun?

TAKE HER, KIND DEATH.

TAKE her, kind Death, take all the mortal part,
Consume the clogging robes that round her cling,
Unlock the fleshly gyves, so wearying,
And lift the suffocation from her heart!
We, who have watched the chill of anguish start,
Have had no vital balm, no offering
So healing as thy subtle touch could bring;
Most merciful of all her friends thou art.
Ah woe! that such unfit, mis-serving shell
Could cage that crystal, wingèd thing—her soul,

Beating its prison bars rebelliously;
Yet joy! for Death's unfailing miracle—
Kind Death, whose other name is Love-in-
    dole—
And that she is alive and soareth free!

SONNET.

WITH A BUNCH OF ARBUTUS.

DEAR Heart, these flowers that I offer you
Shall stand for emblems of you; shy and sweet,
Modest and tender-hearted, fresh and true,
They come, the harbingers of life, to greet
The spring. Securely in their low retreat
They bloom, beneath the dead leaves and the dew,
To tell us winter's rule is obsolete,
And the glad year in hope is born anew.
So into life's drear, wintry days, oppressed
With sordid cares, and worn with hidden pain,
You come like the arbutus flowers, dressed

In spring's dear tones, to bid us hope
   again.
You touch your full, fresh nature to all
   cares,
And who beneath your smile shall think
   of tears?

SUMMER MIDNIGHT.

SILENT the slumb'rous field and forest
   lie;
Silent the hamlet with its human freight;
Only the cricket's chirrup, that so late
Doth keep at his midsummer revelry.
Silent and scintillating far on high,
Ciphers of love that beggareth scale or
   date,
The countless stars sit panoplied in state
Against the dusk, illimitable sky.
Peace, solitude and dark,—and I alone,
Alone in all the glory worshipping!
I hear upon the stillness, one by one,
The midnight hours musically ring.
A day is born, a day is dead and done;—
Darkness and death whereout the dawn
   shall spring.

AMONG THE MOUNTAINS.

THOU 'RT like the mountains, love; these haughty heights
  That sentinel our valley, as a guard
Of star-eyed Titans, whose strong footstep frights
    The hidden deeps as it drops earthenward,
Yet whose great brows do seem to lift the sky;
Who nurture in their bosoms tenderly—
Warm with a mother's touch—the mystic hum
    Of wingèd things, the fountain's throe of birth,
The wedded fragrances that overcome
    The sense, and all life-essence of the earth.

O most mysterious mountains! How full oft
  I watch them, staunch yet swept by change on change!
How loves my brooding soul to search aloft

And find them always same yet always
    strange!
Lo! how their wooded limbs a little while
Do seem to stretch themselves and drink
    the smile
Of the warm sunshine poured in every hid
    Recess and shade; they have no secrets
    now,
But, like a waking infant, lie amid
    The strenuous warmth of their own
    living glow.

How frown they now, when the stern storm
    down-broods
    Darkling with savage and unutterable
    thought,
And all the purple steeps and solitudes
    Sweeps into sullen blackness, over-
    wrought
Of coming woe! Through many a forest
    gap
Strange voices moan and moan; now
    tossed boughs snap,
And great trunks writhe and shudder, as
    the hush
    Is broken by the tempest's furious rout;

The engulfing, wind-driven cloud, the roar, the rush
  Of whirlwinds;—and the hills are blotted out!

But I have known them in a tenderer guise
  When filmy, rose-tipped mists engirdle them,
And on their peaceful breast the long day dies,
  With twilight zephyrs whispering requiem.
There is a lucent shimmer through the air
That scarce is light, yet ever seems to wear
Semblance of light, from the far, rock-crowned crest
  That the departing sunbeam last hath kissed,
To where the valley nestles into rest
  Through a still dream of pearl and amethyst.

Now soft the dusky-robèd Night down-slips,
  And all the land with mystery she drapes.

Within the solemn, shadowy eclipse,
   The mountains wait — vast, elemental
      shapes—
Expectant, underneath the heavenly dome
That overspans in measureless mono-
      chrome,
Where, one and one, on altars all unseen,
   Strange lights do glimmer forth; till, bit
      by bit,
The void is diademed with starry sheen;—
   And in the temple all the lamps are lit!

AN IDYL OF JUNE.

LIE here with me amid the grass,
   Up-gazing through the trees,
And watch the clouds in solemn mass
Like a processional pass and pass
   With snowy draperies.
And we will breathe the waftings pure
Exhaled from locust bloom and clover,
And tinier, grass-enfolded flowers,—
Steal out their souls and make them ours;
   And in their forfeiture
Of self, new self discover.
   The bees shall lull us,

      As here and there they drone
      With drowsy undertone
   From sweet to sweet, shall dull us
Into harmonious tune of perfect hours.
The lordly wind shall sweep our faces
   As if he only grudging kissed
A human lip ere to wild spaces
   He fled to keep immortal tryst.

Not so fast, sweet wind, hie thee not,
The sprites of the air will spy thee not,
   Nor the elves in the thickets harry;
Thy dryad will sure deny thee not,
   If a half, half moment thou tarry
With the snows of thy pinions to fan us,
Where, high and high, in the sky, over-
      span us
   The arches of locust trees.
   The sun shall brood down as it please,
Till the delicate foliage glisters
In golds and bronzes, mate to mate,—
Till the whole wide arch is irradiate
   With tremulous, fairy vistas!
   And the little leaves dance,
   And the little leaves glance
   With their heads askance,

An Idyl of June.

In a soft sun-dance;
And quiver and gleam and droop and shimmer
Against the radiant skies,
As if ripe June had quaffed him a brimmer,
And let the sun-fire through his eyes
Leap out, to rule all the world June-wise!

In the god-commune,
When the gods made June,
They undertook
To utter the perfect thought.
When they made the trees and shook
The dawn through the bloom, they wrought
Better than man conceives;
For they left their spirit caught
In the heart of the locust leaves.
And they laid a spell on the solitude
That never a black world-taint
Should fall, and the mind should paint
Only the infinite rest and the infinite good.
Not a breath of the world outside—
Its folly and shame, its strife and pride,
Its soul-flights mocked and its love denied—

Not a breath of the world outside
  Was breathed in our nook;
It is always high-summer noon.
One could almost count, through the dreamy heat,
  In the pulse of the languid land,
    Each soft heart-beat;—
It needs but a touch of the hand,—
  We shall understand.
In our hearts and our charmèd nook
  It shall always reign June!

MY LOVE IS LIKE THE DAWN OF DAY.

MY love is like the dawn of day,
  One tender flush athwart the gray,
A hint of promise far away.

My love is like the nestling bird
Who flies not though its wings are stirred,
Soft tunes its throat yet speaks no word.

My love is like the budding rose;
Beneath the petals, folded close,
The hidden heart divinely grows.

The flower will bloom, the bird will sing;
At noon comes glorious harvesting,—
And I can wait the summer of spring!

CIRCUMSTANCE.

SHE should have answered "No";
   but, low-inclined,
  The shady branches rustled overhead;
They saw, atween the trunks, the river wind,
  And near, the unmowed meadows whispered.
The yellow sky and shimmering clouds seemed wed;
  The sensuous summer wind with soft caress
Swept by and kissed her cheek and left it red;
  So—sudden moved—she turned and answered "Yes."

THE FULNESS OF TIME.

WHEN the seeds were ready, one by one,
Through the earth they broke;
When the bud was ready, lo! the sun
Touched it, and it woke.

When the heart was ready, half a breath
Rent the veil it wore;
When the soul was ready, loving Death
Oped a wider door.

DANUBE BOAT-SONG.

WE row and row,
And as we go
Our choral song deliver;
In state and pride
Our barge we guide
Adown the Danube River.

Behold arise
Through western skies
Great lights to charm forever,

The sunset's beam
Doth paint the stream
Adown the Danube River.

The wind blows chill
O'er marsh and hill,
The sweet lights fade and shiver;
They fade and shift,
And still we drift
Adown the Danube River.

UNDINE'S FAREWELL TO HULDEBRAND.

O LOVE, mine own, farewell — it is mine hour;
  The bird within the hedge hath ceased to sing,
The violet hath bloomed and shed her flower,
  The summer hastes to sweep away the spring.
Yet is the fragrance on the breeze not dead,
Yet is the echo of the song not fled,

For nothing wholly pure can pass away;
  The violet's breath is on the asphodel,
And in the autumn flames the spring's display.—
  O my belovèd one, farewell, farewell!

Of life love is controller and bestower,
  Of death love is the answer and the king!
I leave with thee my love in deathless dower;
  The fateful rounds of time shall ever bring
The perfume of the flower to thee unshed,
The glory of the dawn untarnishèd;—
For thou art ever mine! Though I obey
The outward touch, my soul doth with thee stay,
  For love is life-in-love inseparable,
And not the fervid dream which lasts a day.—
  O my belovèd one, farewell, farewell!

THE PARCÆ.

> "I hear the Parcæ reel
> The threads of man at their humming wheel,
> The threads of life and power and pain."
> —EMERSON.

SPIN, Sisters, spin! From blossom to decay;
From dawn to night, in perfect counterpart;
Through passion and denial, peace, affray;
 Through love, and pain its twin;
Through conquering weakness; through destroying strength;
And every pulse that rules the human heart
Mete out to each his pre-ordainèd length.—
 Spin, Sisters, spin!

Spin and then cleave. Why should our touch relax
A faintest jot for any seeming jars
Of lower spheres, whose frail convulsions wax
 To wane as naught had been?

For we, the embodying measure of the law,
Standing impassive on the eternal stars,
Behold the perfect sequence evermore.
     Spin, Sisters, spin!

Why should we pause ? Mote in an universe,
Man dreams to shape the ages as they move
To his own ends,—create—subdue—disperse,—
 And, like a harlequin
Of Time, gaze inchwise through the mystic murk;
And set a cipher here or there to prove
Immutable law his puerile handiwork.
     Spin, Sisters, spin!

O self-befooled! Withholden are his ears
From the high thunders that attune his earth
Unto the choiring of rolling spheres
 In vast, supernal din.
Law shapeth him — compelling — passing by;
His very essence law;—or seeming birth,

Or seeming death, alike of mystery.
      Spin, Sisters, spin!

He is and is not. Wind-swept vapor-drift
Across the bosom of a mountain chain—
Wherethrough great peaks their frowning,
 fronts uplift,—
 That, shivering out and in,
Melts and is gone. And fountains downward lave,
And, o'er the crags that unsubdued remain,
Frail flowers spring, and mighty forests wave.
      Spin, Sisters, spin!

In shifting semblances and changeful form
The Eternal fashioneth; naught may
 endure
Save the Eternal. Worlds on worlds of storm
 Sweep not a breath within,
Where the life leapeth in a flame divine,
Enfolded in its protean garniture,
Till Thought arise to penetrate the shrine.
      Spin, Sisters, spin!

There is no new nor old. 'T is Thought unlocks
The chambered labyrinth; with slow success
Reading the oracle in paradox;
   Learns where all things begin
They find completion too; the circling Light
Evoking Entity from Nothingness
To move—and change—in order infinite.
                Spin, Sisters, spin!

There is no new nor old; and Time clasps hands
With Time across the lapsèd centuries.
Thought evermore with kindred Thought commands,
   Fits end to origin;
And æons rolled o'er dead that is not dead
Sift but the ashes—let the Phœnix rise!
Then spin—and cleave—the temporary thread!—
                Spin, Sisters, spin!

A SYMPHONY OF THE HILLS.

THE radiant midsummer days with all their wealth are here!
There is a virtue in the time, a spell upon the year.
The sun on charmèd orbit his appointed period
Doth run, his largesse flinging like a charioted God.
There is a glory in the dawn no other season knows,
A grace upon the eventide, a largeness of repose,
A fulness in the ardent toil that brings the night too soon,
A zest that makes the sinew strong and keeps the heart in tune!

As one upon the margin of some sequestered pool,
Within its watery mirror—placid and wonderful—
In idle mood a stone should cast and watch the eddies break
With ever-widening circles, each swift to overtake

The ripple of remoter ones till lost beyond
   the gaze;
So, from near, over-towering heights to
   where the mellow haze
With tints of evanescence the pearlèd dis-
   tance fills,
Lie, heaped in glad confusion, the multi-
   tude of hills.

They lie in smiling company, and hold
   within their arms
A world of nestling villages and breezy
   upland farms.
Here, miles of sombre forest in blue-black
   shadow sleep,
And, yonder, wastes of pasturage the
   broken hillsides sweep.
How fair, in genial sunshine steeped, lies
   every furrowed row
Of harvest-laden tillage land! And, lazily,
   below
Outspread the dappled meadows, wherethrough with shining trail
The brawling mountain rivulets wind down
   the intervale.

Across a waste of azure, in many a shimmering rift
Flushed by the warm, midsummer suns, the idle vapors drift
And drift in spumy masses that merge and redivide,
Like flecks of foam upcast from some remote and refluent tide.
How from the far horizon the shifty, sensuous breeze
Stirs with its pattering whisper the leafage of the trees,
And toys with myriad sunbeams that flickering downward fling
A maze of golden broidery on the greensward carpeting!

The meadow-lark, rejoicing, springs from his hidden sedge,
While the sparrow's cheerful greeting wakes every wayside hedge.
What chorus in the orchard!—hear how the measure trolls
From vireo and bluebird and golden orioles!

The robin in his arrogant and anxious fatherhood,
Chirps noisily from branch to branch to lure his callow brood;
And through the shadowy forest amid the twilight's hush,
Breathe, like a last thanksgiving, the flutings of the thrush.

The cattle grazing on the slopes beneath the searching sun
Draw down into the bosky dells and hollows, one by one;
And where, with purling undertones through many a ferny nook
And web of flag and flower-de-luce, low sings a little brook,
They, drinking, tramp the muddy marge, then midway in the stream
Stand fetlock deep with drowsy eyes and ruminating dream;
Until athwart the umbrage the farm-boy's call is heard,
When they wind adown the grass-grown lane, a placid homeward herd.

The unctuous soil a treasury reveals of
    coming crops;
Already high the nodding grain the tender
    grass o'ertops;
Here vetch low-droops, full-fruited, folded
    in shining sheath;
There clambering beans festoon their poles
    with wild, luxuriant wreath.
And lo! where lines of lusty corn—a ban-
    nered army—stand,
While lush and trailing esculents lie rathe
    along the land.
All lustful for possession, ill weeds against
    them grow,
But there's Nemesis upon them, with
    swift-avenging hoe!

O acres of wind-shotted and undulating
    grass,
Your sentence is upon you,—I see the
    mowers pass;
While up from every meadow where the
    bobolink sang blithe,
I hear the swish of following swaths, the
    music of the scythe.

The cocks are raked or shaken sheer with
    dext'rous overplay,
And all the air comes laden with the scent
    of new-mown hay;
Till through the lengthening shadows,
    drawn by the stolid ox,
The wain, high-piled with harvest, sedately
    creaks and rocks

Adown the sinuous highway: and home at
    last is here,
A cottage nest betwixt the hills, a harbor
    of good cheer.
The ample barn is fragrant with the breath
    of champing kine,
As the milker with his pail and stool wends
    up and down the line.
Outside the generous door-yard spreads,—
    a wealth of velvet green
Crowned by the over-arching elm that six-
    score years hath seen,
Where the farm-folk from the amplitude
    and well-filled tasks of day
Shall gather in the gloaming to watch the
    children play.

O dwellers in the fetid towns, cramped by
    your sordid need,
The breath of wood and pasture land shall
    make you live indeed!
A pavement is no resting-place for worn
    and weary feet,
They need the fresh, elastic sward, the
    touch of blossoms sweet.
Arise and claim your freedom, shake off
    the servile dust,
And take your place in Nature's arms,
    compelling and august.
What though the labor still seem long—the
    guerdon hardly won?
No man is really poor who owns the fresh
    air and the sun.

She shall not give you unearned gifts nor
    hoards of useless gold,
But every day the miracle of budding
    things unfold;
And every day in stintless light, in rushing
    winds confest,
And deep, inevitable growths, her God
    make manifest.

Your franchise shall be space to breathe
and motive to expand
In body and in spirit, till both shall understand
Her open book, where all may read in
singleness of heart
Of beauty and of love and life without a
slur of art.

Betwixt the verdure-robèd earth and man,
her child, a bond
There is—a fine affinity, which unto things
beyond
Material ends of toil attains, and links him
fast and sure
Through the semblances that pass away to
the meanings that endure.
He hears the deep evangel that underlies
all toil,
The word that breathes alike from winddriv'n cloud or procreant soil;
The dawn bestows a promise that the dewy
night fulfils,
And life grows sweet beneath the benediction of the hills.

GO NOT, LONG SUMMER DAY.

GO not, long summer day, oh, go not yet!
   Spread out your wings for me a moment more!
The sedges with the flooding tide are wet,
   The sunset links the river shore to shore.
Across the uplands birds are twittering still,
   Home-coming kine are lowing far away;
Their destiny and mine thou must fulfil
   Ere thou depart,—oh, linger still, sweet day!

Faintly I hear the far, far village bells,
   Scarce note the passing shadows on the shore;
With me nothing against the silence tells
   Except the quiet dipping of the oar.
A look — a clasp of hands — a rushing thought
   That needs no words to read it as I may,
And oh! my heart the sunset hues has caught!—
   Then linger by me yet, belovèd day!

TO A ROSE CAST UPON A STREAM.

DRIFT by, sweet flower, drift by, fair flower,
  Borne purposeless upon the tide;
Because I clasped thee for an hour
Against my heart and felt thy power,
  Shall but thy thorn abide?

Thy perfume, vague and dream-beset,
  Could not remain unshed a day;
In thee the thorn and bloom were met;
The love and pain, both, I forget;—
  Lie there and drift away.

MONADNOCK CROWNED.

SAVAGE supreme and lone, he reared his head—
  A darkling shape — through the thin upper air;
  His drapery the conifers, but bare
The great brow gloomed, stern and rock-filleted.

Clustered around the lesser hills lay spread,
  Dwarfed by his greatness, and, all unaware,
  Seeming to shrink aside and leave him there,
A regnant presence—beautiful and dread.
  Like some immense disfeatured tapestry,
Shorn of its splendors, neutral-hued and dull,
  The great cloud-weftage hung against the sky
In moveless mass, sombre and sorrowful;
  As, shivering with the late wind's unrepose,
  The waning day sped hasting to its close.

Then up the vacuous dusk went gently stealing
  A tender premonition, life-endued,
  Purfling the veil with rifts all glory-hued,
Wherethrough the hidden sun, in broad shafts wheeling,
The fountains of his being swift unsealing,
  Brake like a god; and poured his molten flood

Over the shaggy shape that, waiting, stood
Transfigured 'neath the radiant revealing.
  Down every ridge and hollow fiery mist
Fled with transmuting touches; here to fold
  A mantling film of sun-shot amethyst,
There, leave a frowning precipice aureol'd,
  And all-where grace ineffable disclose,
As the glad day stole lingering to its close.

JETSAM.

AFTER the tempest, chill and wan and gray,
  Awearily came dawn. Still, dusky-dense,
  The gathered vapors like a pall immense
Blotted against the hid horizon lay,
Where with a moan the spent winds sank away.
  Huge weltering surges, sated with a sense
  Of outworn rage, in turbid refluence
Heaved heavily, with fitful gusts of spray;

  Or flung foam-wreaths along the crinkled
   sands,
Where — past all storm or lull or vital
   needs —
  Lay, face upturned, and stark, close-
   clinchèd hands,
A human form amid the ooze and weeds.
  While, as with shy, mute requiem for the
   dead,
  A single gull swept softly overhead.

EVENSONG.

CLASP hands, Love; wherefore should
  we fear
  To travel down the twilight way?
We who through many an arduous year
  Have jointly borne the heats of day?

There comes a peace at eventide—
  A calm which floods the waiting soul
With images so vast, so wide,
  It cannot yet perceive the whole.

A calm which deeper insight brings,
  And where the heart no longer strives,

For, through the passing of all things,
  We know, we know that love survives.

Clasp hands!—our goal is manifest.
  The sweet lights fade across the lea,
The wind sleeps on the evening's breast,
  The ebbing tide slips to the sea;—
                So we—so we!

PROGRESSION.

WHEN my time comes, may I so gently pass
  I shall not stir this life-round wonderful;
Like flicker of soft wind o'er summer grass,
  Or dip of pebble dropped in some deep pool.
May the white clouds, high-piled, drift slowly o'er,
  Pregnant with inspiration, and so take
My winnowed spirit to some farther shore,
  Nor leave behind a silence nor an ache.

Lament me not, belovèd, shed no tear
  Because of cession of the finite powers;

Lay only happy thoughts upon my bier,
  And hope and love, which are immortal
    flowers;
Knowing I have departed not, but thus
  Do but assume a finer medium
To make a little space more luminous
  For thy dear feet to tread when thou
    dost come.

VESPERS OF THE HERMITS.

AT evening, through the twilight's soli-
  tude,
With the environing hills all worship-
  ping,
Within the border of a little wood
  I heard the thrushes sing.

A lonely place it was, scarce ever trod
Save as some shy four-footed creature
  stirs;
A solemn temple, consecrate to God
  By His own ministers.

Into the bosom of a wind-swept glen
The hillside dropped, precipitously sure;

Therein might timorous creatures have
   their den
  And wild things hide secure.

Below, beyond, receding crest on crest,
Like frozen billows of some upheaved
   sea,
Each farthest one o'ertopping all the rest,
  In savage majesty

The panorama of the mountains swept
To the horizon; forest-clad and dark,
Save where some naked crag might inter-
   cept
  The line with inverse mark;

A wild, untutored waste, through whose
   still air
There swept enfolding, uncontaminate
   spells,
With ceaseless incense rising unaware
  From Nature's thuribles.

Long lingered I in errant musings wrapped,
Dusk as the shadows and as profitless;
Scarce a wind-whisper passed or dry twig
   snapped
  In all the wilderness.

From far away the mountain torrent's voice,
Subdued by distances all foliage grown,
Its hoarse bass softened to harmonious noise,
   Rose like an organ tone.

The sombre hemlocks all around outspread
Their aromatic arms in benison,
While from the netted branches overhead
   The thrushes, one by one,

Broke through the waiting silence with their notes,—
Long, liquid, perceant,—fluting call to call
Mysteriously, from shadow-shrouded throats;
   In sweet antiphonal

Chanting the long day's sacramental hymn.
And as the unearthly cadence rose and fell,
All outward consciousness appeared to swim
   In some dissolving spell

Where form and semblance seemèd to depart
In a still prescience of Omnipotence;
An answering vibrance stirred within the heart,
  A deep responsive sense

Of the supreme antiphony, — dimly showed: —
And through my being sudden rapture clove,
Effused in aspiration, overflowed
  Of wondrous peace and love.

SATTVA.

THE PRAYER OF SILENCE.

I AM a sleeper in a dreamless sleep,
  A leaf afloat upon a starlit sea,
  A lotus-blossom folded silently,
A drop of dew slipping from deep to deep
Of bliss that is repose superlative,
  With neither birth nor death nor day nor night
  But only life in order exquisite.
O God, my Sea, in thee I merge—and live!

FLY, MY SONG.

FLY, my song,
  Swallow-winged that thou art!
On thy pinions strong
Compass the land and the sea,
Searching unfalteringly,
And, wherever she bide or be,
Find me the twin of my heart.

No world so wide—
Wherever she bide or be—
  Mine own can hide.
Were it measure of mountains massed,
Or oceans between us cast,
She must be mine at last,
She must rise and answer me!

NIGHT PIECE.

INTO the night I cast my song;
  Stars in the firmament glistened,
Great winds tossed it, swept it along,
  Not even the dull earth listened.

Over the cadence a tremor of pain
  Dragged with a discord's jar,
And my heart it broke in that low refrain;—
  For how could a song reach a star?

UPON A ROMANZA OF SCHUMANN.

Dreams! Dreams! What panoply of dreams
  Sweep with their shifting sceneries over me!
As if one heard the purl of mountain streams
  Mixed with the diapason of the sea,
The while the theme moves tenderly and seems
  In deeper peace with every harmony.

Upon emotion's wingèd thought I fare—
  As eagles sweep the mountain crags and scars—
Which, like a fairy vision, unaware
  The portals of the unutterable unbars.
My spirit floats into the upper air
  And hears the *Gloria* of the morning stars!

A SONG FOR NOVEMBER.

GONE are the summer days!
   Above the wintry hill
  The north wind mutters chill;
  Cowslip and daffodil
Have gone their ways.

The sun's engendering shaft
  Seemeth to peak and pine,
  Wasting without a sign,
  Like some immortal wine
All spent—all quaffed.

Bleak through the pastures bare
  The shrivelled seed-wings scud,
  There is nor leaf nor bud;
  Life holds in desuetude
The senile year.

And 'mid the forest lone
  Great trees lift branches high
  Naked against the sky,
  And rattle, moan, and sigh
In undertone.

Alas for wind-born words,
  Swift interchanging thought

And heart-beat which hath caught
The summer's glow unsought;—
Fled with the birds!

For what fond will should stay
The wasting of the flowers,
The waning of the hours,
Or chain with human powers
Dead yesterday?

Soon, soon from regions frore
The northern blast shall leap,
With icy besom sweep,
And cover chill and deep
The shrunk earth o'er

With its enfolding pall;
And Nature's frozen night
Fall like a spirit-blight,
Outspreading pinions white
Silent o'er all.

NEVER TO KNOW.

NEVER to know
   Whether he perished by forest or floe;
Whether he sank 'neath his gathering
   stress

And slowly—slowly the pulse grew less,
Yielding its agony throe by throe,
Or whether one short, sharp, merciful blow
Swift set him free while the birds still
 sang:—
Ah, there's the pang—
Ah, there's the pang of it!—never to
 know!

Never to know
Whether he thought of one then at the
 end!
Called for his friend,
Longed for a word or a cooling touch
That could lift so much,
Or a presence only—a vital sense
Of companionship into those shadows
 dense,
To steady him through them;—this he
 might crave
From a heart that could break for him—
 break but not save.
Ah, dear God!—never to know!

TO-MORROW AND TO-MORROW AND TO-MORROW.

AT night I said, "To-morrow he will come,"
So through the night I held my sorrow dumb.

And when at last burst forth the mocking light
I whispered inly, "He will come to-night."

But day and night have passed, and still—and still—
Only the heart-break and the mortal chill.

LIKE A LUTE TOUCHED BY FACILE FINGERS.

LIKE a lute touched by facile fingers,
　Through some dim vista of a vanished past,
To melody ethereal that lingers
　Immortally, and will not be out-cast;

So, through the chill and cloistered chambers
  Of thought, within my being swept along,
Quick with the longing which fore'er remembers,
  Thine image lingers in a deathless song.

TRANSMUTATION.

    " Arise!
Thou shalt mourn no more," said Life;
" I will still thy deep heart-cries,
I will lay my hand on thy strife.

    " Not long
Till the tempest beat to the calm;
Make thy great love into a song,
Lift thy sorrow into a psalm."

SWALLOWS AT SUNSET.

WITH gleaming bosoms lifted high,
  And poised on strong exultant wings,
They circle down the sunset sky
  To happy twitterings.

Swallows at Sunset.

With every facile turn and wheel
   The rose-gleams paint their amber throats,
And flash a hundred glints of steel
   Back from their burnished coats.

Now, in a span that balks the sight,
   They sweep o'er hill and marsh and main,
Then, with their swift and joyous flight,
   Lo! they are here again!

Or low or high it little recks,
   Or far or near it is the same,
Their rapid undulation flecks
   The world with hints of flame.

O fair and tireless ones, my thought
   Doth chafe within its fleshly bond;
I too would rise, impeded not,
   To the serene beyond.

I too would breathe the finer breath
   That fills those realms of upper air,
Uplifted by a wingèd faith
   Which sheds the sordid care.

Oh touch me, change me, lift me high
  Into thy regions of delight;
And let me sweep the sunset sky
  Up to the Infinite!

GOING OUT WITH THE TIDE.

I WOULD slip out to the violet sea
  In the arms of the ebbing tide;
I should rest silent and satisfied
Wherever it carried me.
For the streams low-run,
There 's a westering sun,
And the day is done.

Over the marshes' sweep
With their billowy ranks of reeds,
Masking the runlets deep
And a wealth of amber weeds,
The tide seems half asleep;—
Seems holding the heart like a mirrored star,
Where the visions of day reversèd are,
And the faint ideal
That trembled afar

Going Out with the Tide.

Groweth the real.
Heats of the noon abate,
And the senses wait
In a trance co-ordinate;
For the tidal pulse is calm at the ebb.
And oh! through the marshes' web,
And oh! through the sea-fed rill
The waters sink and sift
As they out to the open drift
Serene and still.
Never an eddy, never a whirl,
Only a soft, white, dimpled curl
Wreathing the weeds with a carcanet,
Leaving them gem-bestrewn and wet—
Leaving a pearl.

Hushed on that mighty breast—
The breast of the violet sea—
Never a care could follow me.
I should lie at rest,
Even to know
There were wreckage below—
Record of tumult and woe,
For above
There is record of love.
A Heaven o'er-arches the place;

In its boundless grace
Springs the measureless span of space.
It is azure o'erhead,
Then flushed to a rosy red
That pales with a protean glow
Till 't is opal transfigurèd—
Till 't is amethyst.
And is it the sky or the sea?
Is it wave or mist?
Far away there 's a mystery.
Oh, farther than sight may go,
There 's a mystery!—
The gracious bow
Of the skies bends low
And blends with the violet sea!

ALLEGRO GIOJOSO.

OH! the young heart in the young year,
    And the thrill of blossoms breaking,
The white cloud over the azure clear,
    And the glad new earth awaking!

Burst, little bud, from your shrouding hood!
    A fair pale garment spin you;

Allegro Giojoso.

I am brother of wild and wood,
   I am blossoming in you!

Sing, dear bird, in prodigal youth
   Your broadcast raptures flinging!
I am one with your vernal truth,
   For my heart is singing—singing!

And, oh! white sun on your radiant round,
   Send legioned sunbeams glancing
In aëry circles over the ground
   To set my light feet dancing!

Blow, winds, blow! from east to west
   Through the wildernesses humming;
There 's a joy in my heart all unconfest,
   For my love, my love is coming!

O glad round world, O fair spring world,
   With your wealth of gracious giving,
I 've an inward miracle unfurled
   Beyond your sweet conceiving.

'T is an opening bud—a pure white flame—
   A song tossed over and over;
For flower and song be all the same
   To the beating heart of the lover.

Oh! the young heart in the young year,
  And the thrill of blossoms breaking,
And the young love that hath no fear
  With the glad new earth awaking!

A SONG OF BLOSSOM.

THROUGH the orchard roaming,
    Where the buds invite,
See my dear one coming
    Haloed with the light!

Apple blossoms o'er her
    Weave an arbor sweet,
While they spread before her
    Carpets for her feet.

Faintly rippled laughter
    Of the errant breeze
Dainty perfumes waft her
    Through the perfumed trees;

And 'mid branches netted
    Stolen sunbeams fall,
All with rose-tints fretted,
    Fair and virginal.

Rosy blooms above her
  Showering o'er her head,
All a world to love her—
  Flushing rosy red.

Through a land enchanted,
  Fanned with charmèd air,
Of divine loves haunted,
  Walks she unaware.

A WIND RUSHED OUT OF THE SEA.

A WIND rushed out of the sea!
  It leapt the dunes on the sandy spit,
And over the surge of waters grey,
Troubled and tossed in the land-locked bay,
It measured its savage minstrelsy
Till the low shores answered it.
    " Waste, waste,
      And care misplaced,
Expectation and toil ungraced,
A snatch at guerdons ephemeral,
And the cry of the spirit under it all!

A Wind Rushed out of the Sea.

      But the world lies free
      Unto me, unto me!"
Sang the wind that rushed from the sea.

With fugitive gusty stirs
It traversed the wild wide marshes o'er—
Marshes pied with russet and gold,
Under the spell of the starlight cold—
And swept to the hearths of the householders,
To break at their very door.
      And their dreams grew black
      With ravin and wrack
Of fleets long-sped but never come back;
Ventures flushed with auroral light,
Void in the vapors before the night.
      For strange dreams be
      In the potency
Of winds that rush from the sea!

O thoughts in the heart of man—
Mingled glory and impotence,—
Ye are the lordly galleons of state,
Laden low with your precious freight,
Sailing a sea of measureless span,
Wafted ye know not whence;

Whirlwind-caught
O'er tracks untaught,
Where will ye harbor, where find port?
I stand on the mystic shores alone,
Question and yearn to the Vast Unknown,
And grasp for the key
Of infinity
From a wind rushing out of the sea!

THE LOST PLEIAD.

CALL to her once again, call her,—
Sister!—
Lest the solemn deeps appall her,
The fathomless abysses
Of the stellar wildernesses;—
Sister, sister!
Ah, wherefore should ill befall her,—
Her, our dearest,
Gone when the night burned clearest?
Not Eos' self is more fair,
When, dewy and dim,
Up through the late night air—
The purple twilight of night—
She pierces the earth's far rim;

Then, rising—rising—
Standeth revealed; from the crown,
Close-wreathed with curling light,
And the lips in a bended bow,
To the delicate foot, half-arched for flight;
The filmy garments scarce disguising
The curve of each shapely limb.
She makes the grim worlds new-born seem,
Surprising
All space with her roseate dream!
Not Eos' self was more fair!
And still it would seem
We might reach her—reach her somewhere.
Is she not there—
There, where remote star-clusters fail?
Or yonder, where nebulæ glister?
Or some meteor, slipped from its socket,
Like a fine, celestial rocket
Sinks in the comet's trail?—
                    Sister, sister,
                           Hail!

Hast thou seen the astral dance?—
The whirling circles of light
That break through the doors of night
As the starry shapes advance?

The Lost Pleiad.

Lo! we were all assembled—
All the seven.
We swept with our candent spark
Over the limitless arc
And lighted the lamps of heaven.
The æthers wavered and trembled;
Planet, moon, asteroid,
The very core of the void,
Took on new meaning—grew bright
At the trail of our garments white.
The universe all was alive—alight,
Tranced with ineffable glory!
Soft airs predatory
Swept our faces with bliss,
Stealing a kiss,
And out of chambered immensity
Awoke all sweet sounds that be.
Mystical, weird night-noises,
Echoes of far-off voices—
The million-throated voices of space,
Like silvery horn-tones answering, calling,
Down through the palpitant ether falling—
Broke in a rhythmic torrent of sound;—
Whispering, rippling, surging, growing,
Upward, downward, over, around;
Till—scarcely heeding or knowing—

We could not choose but dance!
We lifted fair arms to the firmament,
Mingling and swaying in joyous guise;
While from hand to hand stretched a ligament,
A twisted riband of fiery thread,
And over each head,
Flinging its glow in our eyes,
In the band a light was bent—
A single lamp of a star,
Like a fire-opal flashing red
Or the heart of molten spar.
But oh! for the flame in the heart!
The fiery pulse of emotion,
The smile which is rhythm, yet mute;—
Seeming to start
From the aureoled head to the lifted foot
In music translated to motion.
And oh! for the flaming countenance
And out-swept garments curling,
As we circled the midnight's vast expanse,
Whirling, whirling, whirling!
Suddenly,
As if to a signal clapped,
The shining ligament quivered—and snapped!

The Lost Pleiad.

One scintillant lamp unbent,
And, spirting fiery flakes as it went,
Down the endless slopes of night
Vanished from sight.
Over our sister a shadow forlorn
Swept with a swift dilation,
As the hot flame drops to the ash;
We caught a flash
Of startle and consternation,
And then—she was gone!

Weep, Pleione, weep!—
Rent heart and dust-bowed head—
Such tears as only mothers shed
Over their dead.
Sacrifice with us keep,
For thy loveliest one is fled.
And thou, sweet Artemis!
She who hath drunk thy kiss
And followed thy silver feet
With steps more fleet
Than the hunted stag in his heat,
Shall never follow thee more
The breezy hill-crests o'er.
She is swallowed—lost—in the dread abyss!
He too loved her—he of the crusted zone,

He of the belted stars;
Though he sweep the heavenly heights
    alone,
His eyes cleave swifter than scimitars.
Was it his fond pursuit,
His passion following resolute
That snapped the fiery thread of her be-
    ing—
Like a string o'erstrung on a lute—
And drove her, neither heeding nor seeing,
Into the darkness mute?

Cold, cold, cold
Are the awful caverns of space,
And cold, cold, cold
Is the vanished face;
But colder still, at life's lone gate,
The darkened hearts that wait,
No hope—no spark—discerning.
For neither the tender morning light,
Nor the sweet enfolding arms of night,
About the spirit yearning,
Can lift the burden of blight.
And time is not measured by hours—
Following one by one,—
Not measured by orbit of planet or sun,

But by every beat of the anguished heart,
The deadly drip of the wounded part
Which the inward pang devours—
Burning—burning!
And oh! there is no returning
From that darkness inexorable;
It mocks at us, inky—sable;
And our cry through immensity tossed
Goes pitiless echoing, "Lost! lost! lost!"
And yet—once again—
Oh, call to her yet once again!
     Sister, sister!
    Vain—ah, vain!

HYMN TO THE NIGHT.

O HOLY NIGHT, serenest Night,
 Star-filleted and dusky-eyed,
The day aweary of its blight
 Sinks on thy bosom satisfied.

And sordid cares and petty aims
 Fade, self-slain, in that peace of thine,
While newly-kindled altar flames
 Leap in the spirit's secret shrine.

Beneath thy calm immensity
   How narrow seems our daily scope!
Yet how superlative might be
   The circling ranges of our hope!

The earth about our garments clings,
   We sell ourselves for that and this,
And so beneath life's little things
   Its deep, eternal meaning miss.

With outer vision veiled and sealed
   Into a higher sphere we rise,
And catch that vaster life revealed
   By glimpses to the inward eyes.

O World, O Time, the placid Night
   Blots out your fetters with her dark,
And limitations sink from sight
   As of a passing finger-mark.

No more our baffled souls contend,
   The starlight through our darkness gleams,
We dimly feel our final end
   And see the glory in our dreams.

So near, so near, that glory glows
   We know nor loss nor jar nor fret,
But drink this largesse of repose,
   And wait the day which dawns not yet.

AT SUNSET.

LOOK out, dear heart, and watch the kindling sky
   Where great lights flame and vanish one by one;
The western port whence immemorially
   The sun hath beckoned love forever on.

A hundred evanescent pageants melt
   Each over each—wan blues to chrysoprase
That drops in turn to crocus—with a belt
   Of purple hills against the burning haze.

While far across the calm, untroubled bay
   Long-streaming answers trail in ebbing sheen

At Sunset.

Of lesser splendors—orange swept to grey,
   And lilac paling into opaline.

A world of glory which the deeps enhance!
   A world held breathless of the after-gleam;
With soft tides slipping seaward in a trance,
   And little ships adream midway the stream.

There is no room for shadow or regret,
   No place for passion in this panoply,
But sombre thoughts float from us with their debt
   Like cloudy bits of flotsam to the sea.

The tranquil spirit opes its portals wide,
   And visions that too sweet for language seem
Outspread themselves—like this enchanted tide—
   With shining thoughts adream midway the stream.

A TOAST FOR THE YEAR.

PLEDGE me a cup, October,
    Ruddy October!
A goblet rounded and brimming
With sun-shotted wine,
Electric and fine,
The breath of the West o'er it swimming
Like a far-world anodyne.
Lo!
The ardent glow
Of maples—scarlet, saffron, and gold;
The mingled tints untold
That mantle the marshes, scrub and sedge,—
Russet heart with a flaming edge;
Sumacs incarnadine;
Oaks in their draperies old—
Purple and bronze austere;
All things brave and compelling
Shall burn in this luminous wine,
This vintage of all the year.
For thou like a prober
From Earth's secret store
The deepest and purest dost draw
For thy sweet distilling.
Come pledge me a cup, October!

A Toast for the Year.

In the season's brooding lull,
With long low shadows streaming,
The haunted woods are full,
The covert nooks are teeming
With mystery wonderful.
Motes that rise
Through the circling light
Materialize,
Take form, grow bright.
I catch the beat,
The rhythmic swing
Of myriad feet,
Of gossamer garments flickering
Like the flash of a dragon-fly's wing.
Film-attired
Naiad, Oread, Dryad,
Divinities
Of the rivers and rocks and trees,
Down the far, o'erarching vistas,
Through filtered lights advancing,
They come—the airy sisters—
Serenely dancing—dancing.
Twinkling feet to the sunset west,
Fret of the flesh they banish;
Dancing the burden out of the day,
Dancing the fear of a fear away,

Dancing the year to its rest.
Now there, now here,
Through the soft empurpled atmosphere,
They flit—they burn—they vanish!
Too glad for a world grown sober.
Ah! pledge me a cup, October!

Full in the effluence mellow
Self will I steep;
Storing the crimson and yellow,
The wealth of prism-swept haze,
The trance of the loitering days,
Deep, down deep;
Where I keep—
Their virtues hid to surrender—
The essence of all things tender.
Glories that flame
Shall be the same, yet not same.
The prodigal shafts of the sun,
In inward crucible caught,
Be transmuted from color to thought,
To promise—promise of pause and renewal,
The gloaming into the dawn over-run,
Existence not dual
But one.
Lo! how, their message delivered,

The dear leaves have shrunken and shivered,
Have answered the sign!
At thy call
They tremble, and scatter, and fall,
Thou masterful world-disrober!
Thine are they all;
Thine—and mine!
Then pledge me a cup, October!

ORPHEUS SINGS.

THRENOS.

DUSK lie the forest and the cold ravine,
   The shadows crawl adown the friendly slope,
There is no longer light where light hath been,
   The iron crag flings back to me my hope.

And the chill night-wind with its sombre moan,
   Which from remotest sorrow seems to start,
Down the dark avenues and alleys lone
   Finds answering echo through my shadowed heart.

It is as if one lifted to his ear
  The twisted shape of some sea-hearted shell,
And through its convolutions seemed to hear
  The torrent of a life immeasurable;—

A passionate rush, a solemn, ceaseless roar;—
  And felt the hurrying surges leap and press;
Yet is not any ocean there, nor shore,
  Only a curlèd mollusk's emptiness.

The world is changed; the world is old, yet stays;
  But like an autumn leaf which hath no goal
I drift adown the melancholy ways
  With frosts of bitter blight upon my soul.

O Love, I call thee and thou answerest not,
  The void is blank—I know not where thou art;

I only know thine image unforgot
  Burns like a sacrifice against my heart—

Its consecrated altar, where no more
  The living flame shall light the advancing years,
While ever at the altar's foot I pour
  The prodigal libation of my tears.

Oh! for a draught of lethe from the springs
That breed oblivion and a drowsy peace,
A numbness of the knowledge of all things,
  A deadly calm wherein I too might cease!

Bring me hemp philters! so that I may dream,
  My best belovèd, that I am with thee,
Roaming once more the hill above the stream
  Which threads th' enchanted valley to the sea;

Glad in the moment; as a glad wild thing
  Basks in the sunshine, drinks the sun-brewed haze,

And wanders without care disquieting
  In happy vagrancy of summer days.

Or else withdrawn into some thicket's shade,
  Fragrant with herbs and sweet earth-harmonies,
Watching the swallows circle overhead,
  Hearing the fitful rhythm of the breeze.

No need for signal or for uttered word
  To seal the spell of union eloquent;
Like lifted petals were our heart-beats stirred,
  With presence only were we well content.

Almost methinks that I might clasp thy hand,
  And subtly thrill to eyes that feed on mine,
As aye related spirits understand
  The quickening thought without an outward sign.

Ah no! it is a dream—thou art not there!
  'T is but a fatuous memory which doth cling

About a phantom fading into air,—
  A breath—a sigh—in space evanishing!

This world hath been too niggard for thy need,
  Thou tender one! or even to shelter thee
Save a brief while; too full of sordid greed,
  Too narrow for a rounded liberty.

My spirit beats its unavailing wings
  Like a caged bird that pants to be set free,
For I in flight would quell all questionings,
  Searching the universe, O Love, for thee.

Not earthly bond should hold me. I would dive
  Into the nethermost deeps and fastnesses,
Probing their darkling ways,—lest thou survive
  Through caverned labyrinth or dim recess.

Or, heavenward-flung, would seek thy
    dwelling-place;
  On lifted pinions cleaving far and far,
To compass vast illimitable space
    Bearing my passionate quest from star to
    star.

O mortal strain for an immortal sight!
  Material semblances not thee contain,
Thou art not in the depth nor in the
    height;
  They mock my hope;—in vain—in
    vain—in vain!

Yet naught may perish. In the abiding
    march
  Through changeful cycles of eternal
    law—
Like veiling vapors o'er the heavenly
    arch—
  The *thou* and *I* endure forevermore.

Arouse thee, my belovèd, answer me!
  For love is not a gift, it is a debt—
An unpaid claim—at deadliest usury,
  Which fast and faster fetters doth beget.

The thought may slip its chains like bird uncaged,
  But in the nest there writhes a brood of care—
Of unfed pangs—that will not be assuaged
  Save only love return to nestle there.

And dark the heart lies,—an unsensing thing,—
  A waiting potency without a name,—
A force whereout the throes of life do spring,—
  Till mighty love shall touch it into flame.

Till mighty love shall touch it into flame,
  Till mighty love unloose the fiery stream
Which none may counterstand and none may tame,
  Which sweeps all being in a burning dream.

Oh! then alone we live! Oh! then alone
  Man stands—a god—upon the mountain crest
Drinking the orbic glory of the sun,
  A greater glory answering in his breast.

Orpheus Sings.

Wilt thou not wake, mine own? and art
   thou then
  In lethargy too pitiless to know
The fervid transport of my song again,
  Or start to life within its overflow?

Art thou too cold to feel the vital breath
  Of love's enkindling spirit breathed on
   thee
With magic inspiration?—and shall Death
Forever hold thee in his mastery?

Art thou too cold—too cold? Still my
   despair
  Lends life to love which heeds nor ban
   nor bar;
If vainly through the living realms I fare,
  Still shall I find thee where the shadows
   are.

Wherever more thou passest—shade or
   day—
  I too will pass. I faint, I fail, I die!
Freed of its clod, the soul *must* find the
   way:—
  Receive me once again, Eurydice!

RHAPSODY.

BEING WORDS TO A PIANO IMPROVISATION.

PLAY to me, Sweet!
   As the wan twilight lingers,
Loth yet entirely to fall
With its pervasive neutral over all,
Making the near remote, the palpable strange,
Will thou a change;
And, like a wizard, with thy puissant fingers
Awaken visions pure and pastoral.
Thy pulse along the senseless wood shall beat,
And while material shades obliterate
The outward world, more fleet
Thou, godlike, shalt create;
And then swift-wingèd thought—
Swift-wingèd thought that knows nor curb nor stay,
Leaping the meagre measure of the day—
People the void with beauty, caught
From inward realms where the world troubleth not.

We shall behold
Vast primal solitudes
All unprofaned by man, serene and full
Of splintered half-lights and low-lying shades:
And wonders manifold
Of murky coverts cool,
And unexpected glades
Fragrant enow for hamadryad's bower
Where, if a wind but stirs
A leaf, a grass-blade or a fragile flower,
One dreams the step is hers:
Of many a drowsy, amber-colored pool
Where idle sunbeams dream away the hour
And a rapt loneliness broods:
Of winding alleys betwixt colonnades
Of aromatic mighty-limbèd firs:—
And all the mystery of the cloistered woods.
Ah! well meseems the little oozy drip
Of nascent fountain which doth slip
Beneath the o'erlying ledge—
Half loitering to toy betwixt the tip
Of clinging ferns and leave them pearled and wet,
Half bold with privilege,
Over the moss and humid polished stones

To gather to a tiny rivulet
That with crooned undertones
Leaps forth it knows not where
So but it find the sunlight and the air,—
Hath caught some impulse that it wots not of,
Some echo whence long branches, over-met,
Make music far above.
Long, long, in-linkèd branches, myriad-strung
With Nature's living wires
Which her warm touch inspires
And which the fitful winds do harp among
In melancholy passion, vague, remote;—
As 't were far-pulsèd note
Of some vast ocean with reverberant roar
Against an alien shore
Hurling itself, to break and fail and fall
In foam ephemeral.
Or else perchance the roll
Of those profounder cadences which lie
Near to Infinity;
The shocks
Of spiritual tides against material rocks,
In ceaseless effort to be free—and whole!

Is then the ivory dowered with a soul ?—
A vital touch to lift the spirit torn
Into a nobler eon ?
Lo! in a moment am I borne
Above this troubled trance
Of place and circumstance;
In joy unknown before
I mount, I soar,
And cleave the empyrean!
Above the empyric wind,
Cloud-wrapped and mist-defined,
Upward, through circumambient airs;
Where, from their fiery lairs
Swift-darting meteors
Break without pause—
Break in coruscant splendor!—
Upward, still upward, in divine surrender!
Celestial space is full,
Boundless, unfathomable.
Star-clusters burn
In ever-widening glories; planets stream
With majesty supernal;
And on ecstatic orbits, vast, supreme,
Rolling from cognizance still to return,
Measurers yet annihilants of time,
Coeval with the Eternal,

Remote worlds gleam:—
Worlds upon worlds, stupendous and sublime!

Nor strifes nor questionings nor fervid stress
Shall mar the measure of my blessedness.
As some still vap'rous weft,
Some sunset exhalation
Trailed o'er a luminous sky,
Doth dream and drift;
So, on the bosom of Immensity,
Serene, fulfilled I lie—
A breath of Aspiration!

THE END.

www.ingramcontent.com/pod-product-compliance
Lightning Source LLC
Chambersburg PA
CBHW020256170426
43202CB00008B/395